THE ART OF AFTERMATH

Tim Maul and Catherine Morris

Words and Pictures Exchanged
between 07/2020 – 03/2023

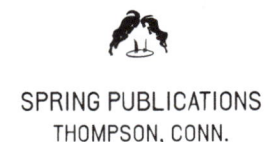

SPRING PUBLICATIONS

THOMPSON, CONN.

Tunnel Visions

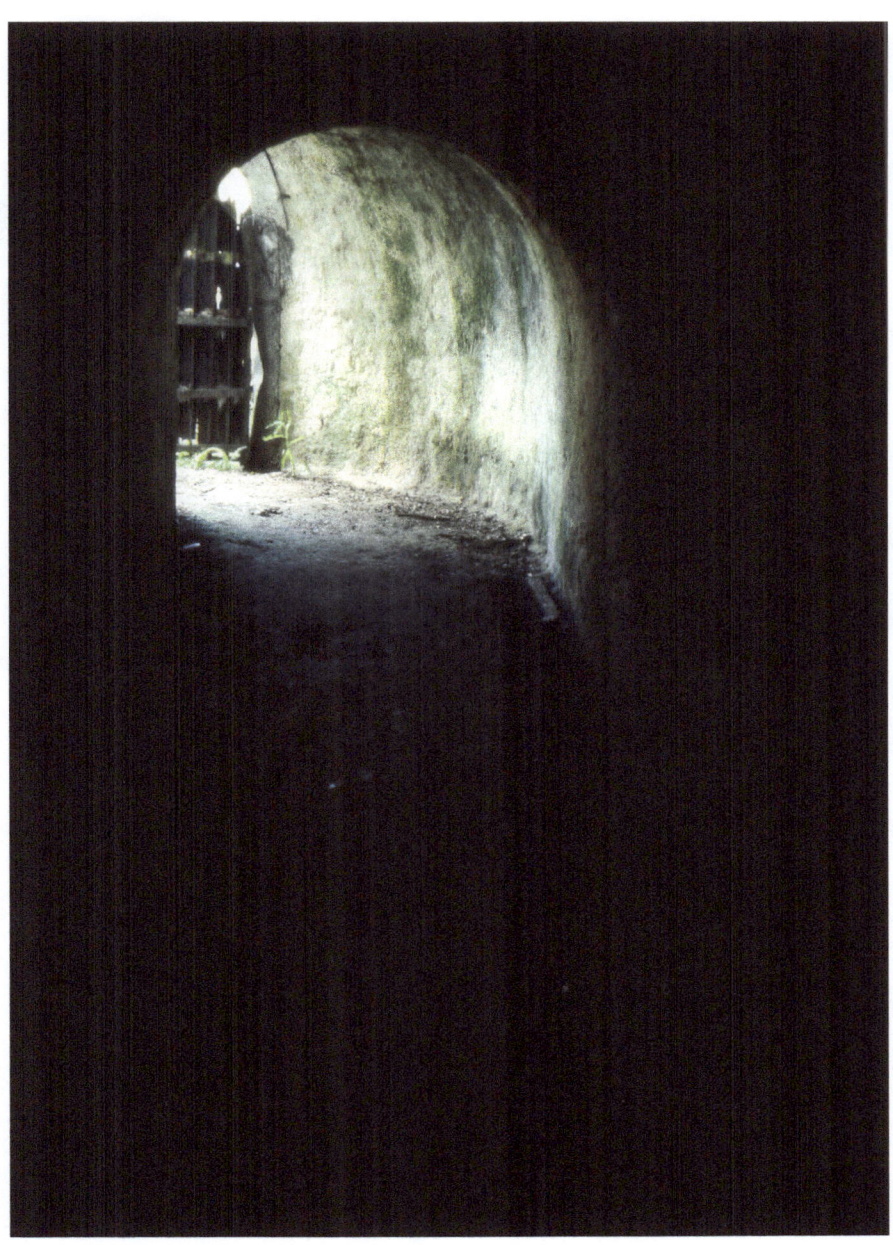

Thank you Catherine Morris for suggesting I readdress these three images I produced late in the last century.

I am on a screen, but let's pretend we're sitting at a large table with a clean surface covered with a sheet of newsprint for additional safety. I have daintily removed the three glossy Cibachrome prints from their individual sleeves and separated the single vertical Irish picture from the horizontal French duo. We'll imagine each print on 11 x 14 inch paper, and because all the photographs are dark, their printed borders require some scrutiny to discern. The lone vertical image on our left clearly shows the gaping maw of an exit from a tunnel, a "servant" tunnel at the National Famine Museum in Strokestown Park. On our right are the two sequential images of a unlit room with a small television image in its upper left corner. It was taken in a hotel in Paris in the Bastille District. The room was as small as it looks here. A young woman's face partially fills the small blue screen, and in the following Tunnel Visions picture she is awoken by a man of color. I may fold my arms on the table and lean in, my eyes flitting between the three positioned shiny rectangles. I have long been satisfied with these images and like any art that succeeds (in that it still holds my interest) they are both mine and someone else's. They shimmer at my touch and elevate the poetic over the ironic or critique, a distinction I was allowing myself after decades of self-policing and tight censorship. The tunnel exit is the more intentional of the trio, reportage with a job to do and a story to illustrate while the French pictures are diaristic with mythic bohemian Paris in evidence and mildly flaunted. I believe that during this visit I attended a panel discussion on Robert Frank at the Pompidou Centre, and to my satisfaction my friend and panelist Beat Streuli referenced me from the stage...so maybe...

Over the previous several decades I had, with some effort, asserted myself into the deeply competitive art world of lower Manhattan while keeping the staid reverential "gated community" of Fine Art Photography at arm's length. Now, in the 90s, sober and with a degree of critical and professional support (an occasional gallery show), I loosened up and brought my camera along when I traveled. During this period I showed my wares to a local gallerist (with whom I would work closely) who bluntly asked "Do you just walk around taking pictures of stuff?" I bowed my head and answered "Yep." I had succumbed, I was now "taking" instead of "making" photographs. The difference is huge.

There is a lite mercantile component to what I do (okay, my practice), and I take note that while beautifully printed, no one owns these images. All three prints are theatrically dark, and I got lucky managing this absence of light to my advantage. Each picture was printed directly from a 35mm slide/transparency by a professional at Clonachrome in Chelsea. Tech bores me, but I used 400 ASA Fujicolor film for its color saturation formed chemically on the tiny segmented surface. Looking at slides today feels clinical as they inscrutably slumber in plastic sheets of 20, and we hold them up to light like a lab technician with a beaker. They are the great-great-grand children of the stained glass window and desperately await conversion into digital files. I will write first about the Irish picture followed by the Parisian photos and end with a few brief thoughts on darkness as represented by the color black.

1) Catherine: Here is a photograph of a bright wound or hole in the picture. It is the entry/exit of the aforementioned servant tunnel, a feature of many "Big Houses" in Ireland and throughout Europe. I visited my friend Luke Dodd founder and first curator of the Famine Museum numerous times since the early 80s and often for weeks. The house, crumbling servant quarters and farm were psychically unsettled and not to be casually explored. I was interested in the banking of gloom in the buildings core and in the books and ephemera abandoned in place as in a volcano eruption or nuclear explosion. Some rooms were impeccably preserved while others were shabby with the majority in total disrepair. A "gymnasium" for the Packenham Mahon family still had graffiti from the British occupation during the war for independence and I once, when helping Luke move some furniture, came across an English edition of *Mein Kampf* from the 1930s. Luke instructed me to toss it and that it wasn't that old. Entropy and inertia prevailed. As a favor I had traveled over one snowy January to photograph the house for an article by Terry Eagleton for *The Observer Magazine* (1994), but I believe this image is earlier and taken

during a previous summer. I found the tunnel appalling and only walked through it once with my camera. Its purpose was aesthetic, to erase the sight of employees from outside views of the house. Didn't Beckett make a film around "to be is to be seen"? (Some smart artist should project this film on the tunnel wall.) I do not remember how it was lit, but I would have remembered torches. It was not long but had a repressive vibe and dank mineral scent, one I haven't recognized since. I did not inspect the wall but it was most certainly brick. A recently repaired green wooden gate (one can hear it creak) is in evidence slightly askew. What exchanges, if any, were shared here? PBS class porn like *Downtown Abbey* mined the intrigues of devoted staff to benevolent family earning a massive following here in monarchy-starved America. I steadied myself and around half way inside I made exposures to both my direct front and immediate behind. Stanley Kubrick had used a Zeiss lens to accurately capture candle and daylight in *Barry Lyndon* (1974), and I remembered this at Strokestown in the peeling hallways only periodically illuminated by a weak Irish sun. While the 35mm format works for the tunnel image(s), it is probably less suited for most of the other pictures. Here the capabilities of a Robert Polidori (Hurricane Katrina detritus) or Perry Ogden (Francis Bacon's studio) would be put to better use making yet more "porn," this time "ruin porn," the glamorization of obsolescence, and a familiar Art School/Photo Fair mainstay.

Tourist guides take note of Ireland's dramatic "sweeping" coastlines, which recede in the agrarian interior that while photogenic (re Jill Uris's controversial *A Terrible Beauty* collection) also may resist contemporary photographic approaches (at least for me, I've spoken to media artist Willie Doherty about this, and he concurs). The other absent tunnel image is of a small set of ascending granite stairs located in the center of the otherwise black expanse. They are clean and maintained, the entry into the house's rear warren of hallways and staircases used by servants alone. I have no jpeg of this image, and they really would look interesting shown together, the degraded (and degrading) opening where "the light at the end of tunnel" does not offer hope, imparted knowledge, or even a possibility of reprise from one's labor. The vertical rectangle is usually reserved for portraiture, and

I use it rarely. if I squint my eyes the opening briefly morphs into a grotesque masked skull with a clenched jawline like the duck/rabbit or Jastrow illusion cited by Wittgenstein. Or maybe I'm just tired and see death in everything.

2) Catherine: Romanticism is heady stuff, and I don't think it will be making a comeback any time soon. Casual photographs of someone may come from a place of romance. In fashion, signaling the romantic can induce self-reflection in those desiring more of whatever the image offers. Sentimentality in league with romance can produce easy-on-the-eye kitsch, and pleasurable examples include Ralph Gibson's Paris images. The factual is never immediately romantic, but can be manipulated to appear so. Engineered romanticism is still romantic. I watched *Titanic* in a motel room during a snowstorm and was surprised on how moved I was. But Kate and Leo had chemistry, so I totally bought their romance. More on "chemistry" shortly.

In favoring the habitual over the random I usually photograph every hotel room I stay in. Perhaps this sanctifies each space like tossing a little holy water around keeping the demons at bay. I organized a exhibition around this work at Leslie Tonkonow Artworks + Projects in New York, and I read the word "ennui" in a review that followed. For those lucky enough to afford one, the hotel room provides the temporary comforts of home when traveling. If walls could indeed talk they would tell of unpacking, sleep, planning, laptop-ing, changing outfits, personal hygiene, and sexual activity of varying degrees. Here the room is very dark with a small television set (!) on a shelf in the upper left half each exposure. An angled shaft of open curtain screams Europe with overcast sky and rooftops featuring skylights. Titled *Paris Sleeps*, it is a sequence of two pictures reading left to right, two of the many I took at that moment. When staying in a hotel I normally perch on the side of the bed and see whats on TV, mastering the remote and clicking (a friend calls this "montage-ing") through sports, weather. news, and especially abroad in the 80s–90s queasy adult scenarios, but I believe the *Paris Sleeps* images come from a French cop show. In the first image, the actor, with collared shirt, appears to be sleeping with a bare suggestion of someone with her. In the following exposure, a man of color enters the screen from above and nuzzles her awake, and she turns to him. This intimate shift is all that matters, Paris still manages a promise of beatnik liberties that resonates with Americans of a certain age.

I am obsessed with sequence and episodic assignations in art for walls and its been a private struggle to justify exhibiting single prints. I want little marriages and conversations between pictures mimicking how cameras once worked, especially in one of the birthplaces of the cinema. I see now that I overlaid basic frame to frame animation (the cinema) over the receptive, fluctuating horizontal tubes of the television, producing a first and next image in real time. All photography is appropriation, and being born in 1951 I am well versed in the second-hand. I watched *The Wizard of Oz* on a small black and white television and listened to the Rolling Stones recordings of Bo Diddley songs. Photographs off of screens have been around since the televised media's development in the 1920s. Robert Frank and Diane Arbus took numerous images off of TVs and at the movies admiring the flow of broadcast images as comfortably seated flâneurs. The TV replaced the newsstand as image trove for artists John Baldessari and, later, John Waters. In the 70s, VCR's, Betamax's and video cameras appeared in studios of savvy upwardly mobile commercial photographers and a few flush artists. For fashion photographers Helmut Newton and the influential Guy Bourdin pre-recorded images on TV's were set for a specific shoot and contributed to their decadent narratives. I gingerly introduced my students to both photographers in a lecture on the 70s and having been exposed to way worse in terms of content (the Internet), they surprised me in appreciating them. I believe when taking the Paris images, it was probably Bourdin that whispered into my ear and, like many in the 80s, I could not wait for his weekly ad for Charles Jourdan shoes in the Sunday supplement of the *New York Times*.

Early screenshots were apparitions that dissolved into each other in electronic purgatories and included the blur, motion historicized in the speed of the film or on the surface of canvas. The blur as visible past was manufactured in paintings by Francis Bacon, Robert Rauschenberg, Andy Warhol, and in Gerhard Richter's "representational" pictures of people and events. (The majority here gay men, why?) Seeing these two small screen images again I take note of the basic features of the woman exoticized in my memory as a somnambulant Brancusi or Art Deco Kiki of Montparnasse. Any hotel room also harbors a backlog of personal histories that we choose to ignore as we snap open our luggage or grab a nap before dinner. These two pictures may operate as voyeuristic time-travel animating the room's recent past, what was happening in the bed below (absent in the darkness) is now relocated on to the screen above.

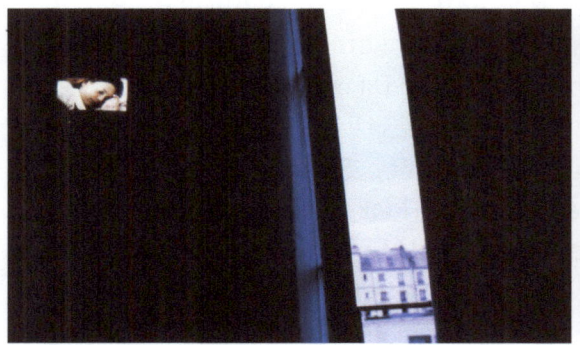 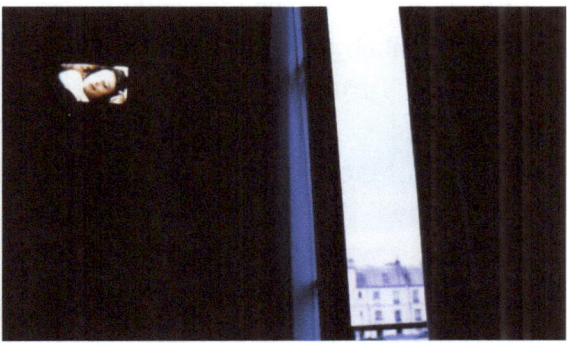

3) Catherine, I recently turned 69 and have been reflecting on how to avoid making the wistful middle-aged art that some artists do, convinced that finally, here's the Real Me, which demands your serious consideration. I've observed that viable living artists (practitioners, I guess) sidestep risky tangents into the personal unlike a pop star's "divorce" or "political" album, which usually disappoint in sales. Camera art may exclude the biographical (studio constructs and orchestrating fictions) or base itself entirely around it (the family documentarian, indisputable truth). Cindy Sherman and Nan Goldin inhabit opposite ends of the spectrum here.

Darkness bonds all three prints of simply composed pictures of a passage's entrance in cruel detail and of flip-book erotics within proximity of a stage curtain awaiting opening onto less-than-gay *Paree.* Printed in black and white, they would not be "warmer" or exceptionally different. These are each clammy voids with their light sources as subject and main attraction. The dark in them is not the color black. If these images were taken with a digital camera, how would they differ? I agree with A. O. Scott's observation in a review of the first *Shrek* movie that the precise surface of pixels held "no refuge" for the eye. Flowing through my prints here are chemicals dissolved into water, a natural element that according to wildly different image makers Nobuyoshi Araki and Jeff Wall transported a "ghost" into the invention of photography. Water diluted with the toxic poison necessary to the Cibachrome process may not introduce an especially friendly ghost.

Black paint or enamel. Best seen in 50s painting and sculpture, early Rauschenberg, late Rothko, Louise Nevelson, Ad Reinhardt, Franz Kline, and Clyfford Still, everything of Tony Smith and Frank Stella, who put the brakes on Ab-Ex's bipolar deal with the devil. Also Warhol's inky tabloid black in his silkscreens and portraiture. Steven Parrino's art described the music he listened to and made. Black in photography? Lilian Bassman's fashion work for sure, deep and luxurious. (I knew her daughter photographer Lizzie Himmel who was behind me at SVA.) And the night in Peter Hujar's 70s images of the Lower West Side of Manhattan was my night too. Consider here the difference between the image on the page and the picture on the wall. In music (again)? No question—James Brown and "Paint It Black" by the Stones ('66), a feverish buzzing mantra notable as a soundtrack to the Vietnam war. I owned the single. Dark enough, I think. I'll pretend to return the three pictures back to their sleeves and put them away.

Thank you again, Catherine.

Tim Maul 08/07/20

In Memory of Michael Maul (1953–2020)

The Art of Aftermath

Freedom alone can account for a person in his totality.
—Jean-Paul Sartre

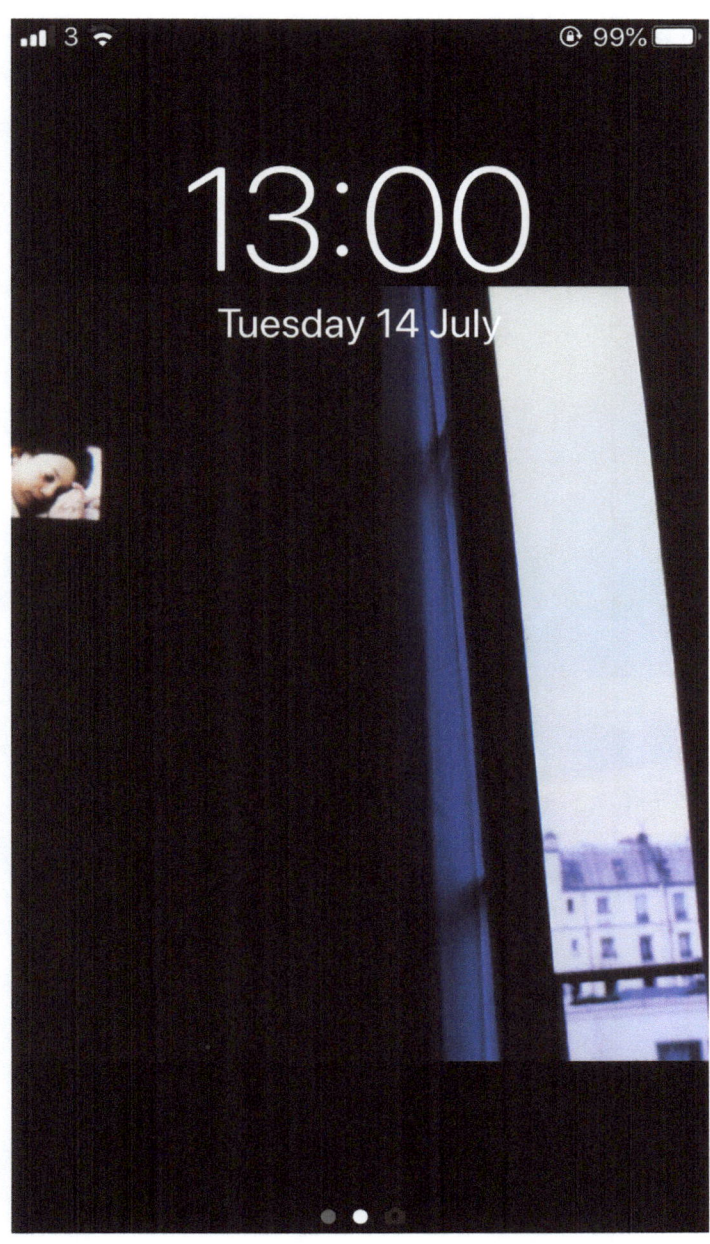

Darkness in a hotel room. A woman is sleeping. A curtain out to a balcony views the tops of apartments in the Bastille. 14 July Bastille day in Galway, and the saver on my phone reminds me of the French Revolution and of Tim Maul's textured darkness. That curving interior tunnel that led workers onto Famine Roads out of Strokestown and into Liverpool. Her dreamings escape out of (or do they come in from) the open window: Paris, the lit version of her unconscious journeying. A TV image of the most private human moment; a woman is sleeping. Is she vulnerable to the stranger's eye separated in darkness from her connections into the open city below? The screen a second pair of eye lids; Tim's camera the third. Eyelids, skin, glass screens and windows. The view from a bed: a woman sleeps on TV and Paris breathes in and out possibilities; longing: did she wait too long? Two days earlier on the 12th July last year, others took their dreaming into the vaults of the celebrated revolutionary dead. Catherine earlier that day had asked: "Where are the women?" as she walked down steps into the underworld. Crossing Hades later that afternoon, another question was asked:

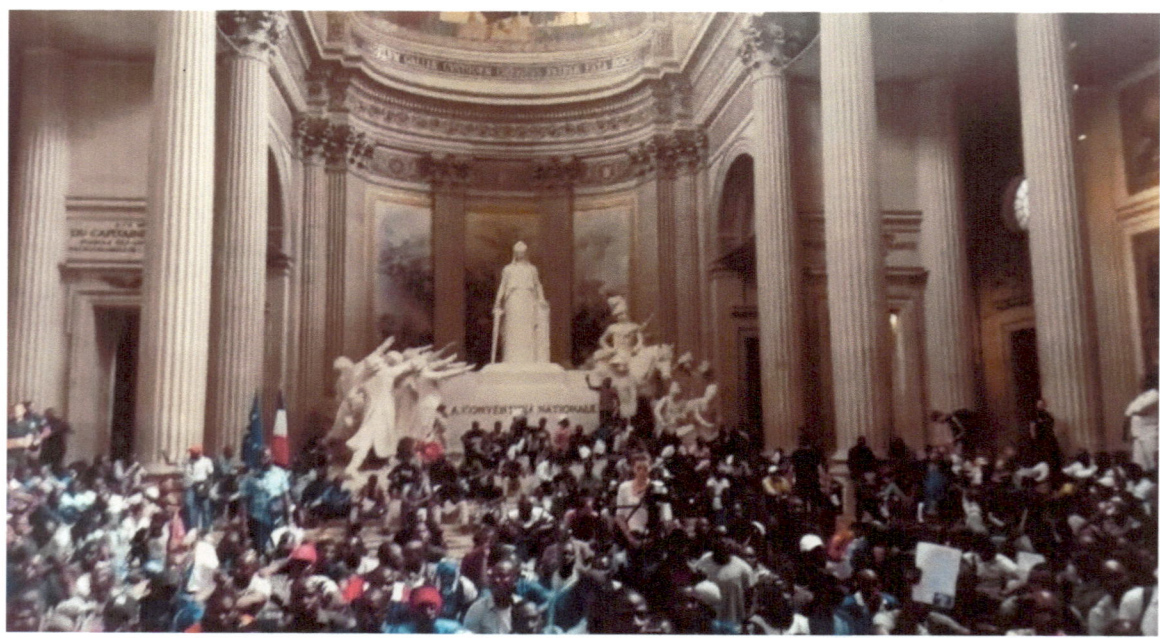

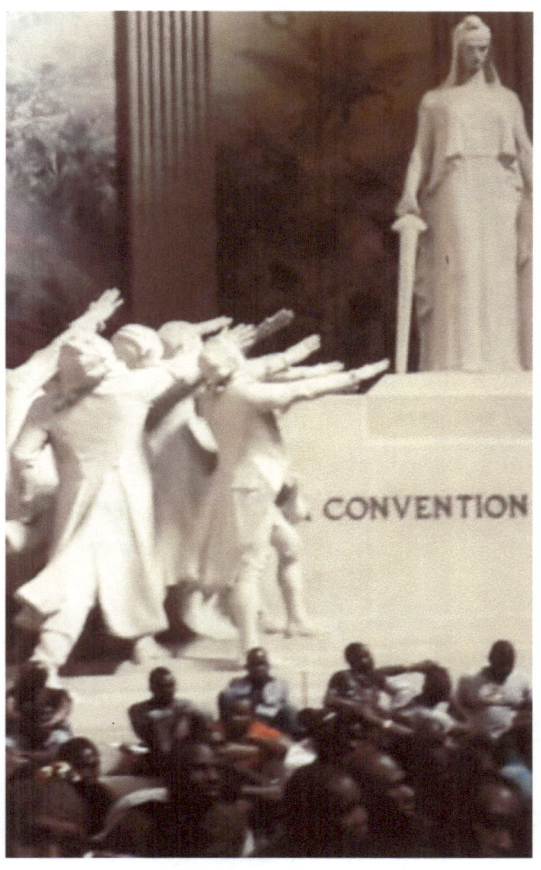

What were the individual conditions that led to this collective action? How would we find out what the people in this picture were feeling as they tried to take control of the contingencies of their lives? What happened next happened behind closed doors. By the early evening undocumented workers had been made to disappear all over again as if by magic. In the North, the Orange Lodge marched. A woman remembered it was her birthday and drank a glass of wine somewhere near the Luxembourg gardens. Tourists returned to the Pantheon at six o'clock and Catherine's question: "where are the women?" was answered but only half understood.

Walking back through our conversation earlier:

"Can you see the snow falling in the background?" "No, I can't see you" I answer, reading your name in the box next to me in my box. The light bulb in my room is broken and earlier I had stood on top of the table to see could I fix it, but I could not and so I talk to you in a darkness lit by Christmas lights and a small torch; irises in the vase still green and not purple, and I am uncertain if they will show at all now that they are dead. In Dublin it is that Spanish time of day *tardes*; for you? Maybe it is mid-morning. You click into view. Snow falling heavy fast live outside a window that looks like it is eighteenth century or Georgian. It reminds me of where I am. A tall house built in 1834. Silk Merchant: the resident here when Famine refugees passed along the canal at the front of the house on their way from Strokestown to Liverpool.

Intersections of our lives that bring us here today. "The confessional" is how you describe the feeling of teaching on zoom. I imagine students in China waking or staying awake for your art class at their 3 am last year. This year. We think about it. Something abstract. That word abstract. The insurrection. "I thought it would come sooner. Happen faster." We pause into the question of not quite knowing what it feels like to stand in that snow outside or to walk into this mild Irish weather. Early in the year; later than we thought.

You tell me you are in Connecticut. "The house where I grew up." I think about the rooms I have never seen and about growing up there and what that might feel like. I try to see the books and the papers and structures behind you. I watch the snow fall fast.

I live in the house where I grew up. But only in the imagination of daily ritual where I sometimes encounter my mother or the ghost of our two selves somewhere back in 70s Liverpool where I have all this double vision of a life not lived and enjoy seeing her then at the age I am now. I ask you about the death of your brother. The piece you wrote in response to the piece that I wrote is an encounter with images, photographs drenched in their own moments and again somehow in grief held in amber; heard in all those sentences.

"Yes, there is a lot of grief in it," you say as though to yourself. In April...and then on June 7th he died. Everything about the circumstances of his death are so painful for you to say and for me to hear. The structures that sustained him. The touch of mirrored water you walked through to get to him to be him to know the thin line that you might cross. February—Aquarius—water carriers bearing the weight of the world. Caring. Carers. "I cared for my parents."

We walk back through the prints of Irish books, the National Library of Ireland. I shine the torch into the negatives you gifted me and try to show you the illuminated stained glass open book—I am amazed at your generosity to me. I am honoured by your gift of these negatives that shine like the jewels they are. A part of my exilic archive that I have carried with me since we last met and through the multiple of lives felt in the blur you mentioned when talking about Gerhard Richter. I hold the negatives to the torch light and catch warm glimpses of book spines, open pages, shelves hidden from public view. Then. Now. A library that is my thinking breathing still moments reading wanting unable to...What they might have been, what they still could be.

Those prints in Ireland. I begin to think about these pictures again as you describe the process of taking them and the difficulty in developing them in Ireland.

Gabriel Byrne reads to us from a recording he sent "for the day that's in it" and the snow falls again on the living and the dead. We remember a hidden daughter whose mother was not "obedient to history". We watch her paint pink lips onto a bathroom mirror. Suspended somewhere north of a communist state of mind we travel to Ireland in 1966 and 1968. "I never took a tourist picture of Ireland." You were never a tourist. I think about all those hotel rooms. Paying attention to what we don't see as we make transitions in time between places that are not home. Ireland: a return journey of kinds for both of us. What did you say about your mother—it astounded me, like encountering an unexpected thread of red cotton or seeing that fox on the church wall at the back of the house the day I moved in. "I didn't trust who she was. I wanted to know"...what was it you wanted to know? Ireland in 1966. Staying at the Gresham. That is what took us to Gabriel reading from *The Dead.* You found a book for James Coleman in Thurles or Kildare and delivered it to him. A test. A provocation. A ritual journey finding your way to the archives of Ireland and that dark tunnel that leads all the way to the revolutionary imagination of the damned, the destitute who are always almost erased.

Catherine,

I switch on the light to find myself in a library. It is the National Library of Ireland in Dublin 1994, and I am downstairs somewhere having been invited to photograph the building and its contents. There are no dead bodies present in that libraries are often the settings for Anglocentric "whodunits" seen on ridiculous fare like *Midsomer Murders,* which has found a home here on local public television. I feel like an intruder, a spy trespassing in some Joycean giants brain, in reality a storage facility for books few people need to interact with for research or personal literary enrichment. It is quiet here, no traffic heard. Brian Eno would be well challenged to compose "Music for Libraries."

I am not sure if Agatha Christie originated the library murder (in her case a library room within a large country house). Even small libraries are labyrinths that often require directional advice from an employee before we organize our thoughts to locate a book or periodical if they exist in physical form. Some individuals choose to read, work, and reside in these public spaces becoming fixtures known to the staff. A library murder inevitably requires the questioning of a prim, bespeckled person who knows next to nothing about the corpse. This individual is usually protective of the institution and often female, both curt and repressed, holding something back which contributes to a form of nerdy allure. John Banville's recent mystery *Snow* (2020) is a sexually twisted Christie exercise that I do not intend to read again for a long time. You'll remember the snow out my window when we Zoomed last month, Catherine.

My project at the NLI came together quickly after meeting Dr. Éilís Ní Dhuibhne, introduced through my curator friend Luke Dodd. She proposed I begin on my next trip to Ireland and that the library acquire selected images for its collection. I was thrilled having frequently photographed books, fascinated with them as titled object, a form of portraiture both individually and in groups. As an artist who works in media I have taught, written criticism, and genially lectured about my art, but I am no scholar of any depth, a prerequisite to what megadealer Larry Gagosian refers to, correctly I think, as "Curator Art." It would be a struggle for me in the unlikely event I'm ever asked to do a Top Ten list at the beginning of *Artforum* or *The New York Times*' intimidating "By the Book" interview(s) with authors and poets.

I brought to Dublin a 35mm Nikon, a basic tripod, small light table, many rolls of Fujicolor film of different ASAs and a loop for viewing slides. I checked into a small hotel that I knew near Parnell Square, and the young woman on the desk, maybe a teenager, asked if I was in "the entertainment business." I decided to tell her that I was.

I cherish books but do not own as many as other artist friends of mine do. I understand that in art they symbolize "learning and knowledge" according to a quick online search. In the mid 90s, during a residency at Lightworks in Syracuse, N.Y., I began hearing ideas around the death of the book as physical object and in the space of the library as one of obsolescence and ultimately neglect. Concurrent to this was the diminishing status of the photograph or any technically produced image as a representation of truth in documenting a place or event. Domestic computers and video recorders as noted by Laura Mulvey in *Death 24x a Second* (2006) had transformed even casual tech users into forensic sleuths enlarging scanned photographs or alternating the motion and speed of videos in ways once only available to professionals with an editing table. In mid 19th-century America, spiritualism flourished in response to magical inventions like photography and the telegraph, while the 90s tech boom saw renewed interest in analog/alternative methods in the darkroom, "primitive" body modification in the form of piercings and tattoos, and later in that decade, popular television packed with teenage witches and awesome vampire slayers. A drifting art market welcomed the occult pageantry of Matthew Barney, increasingly grotesque Cindy Sherman's and prelapsarian Victoriana of photographer Justine Kurland, among others. Also of that moment were the cluttered tableaux in Peter Greenaway's decorous somewhat forgotten cinema, which I found provocative in a British Joel Peter-Witkinish kind of way. Currently, our Wes Anderson is a entertaining sunnier exponent of micro-managed storyboards, art direction, and plot structure.

I arrived at the NLI and was given a basic tour and then left alone. I never used my tripod. The few I encountered paid me no mind, and I was never "shushed" in my silent rounds. I have never been in love with either camera's or the darkroom having labored in sweaty Midtown Manhattan photo labs through the 70s into the 80s. The camera to me still feels like a prop that ultimately dictates both my behavior and the organization of what I see through the lens, it's a passive/aggressive machine.* The Nikon may have been the wrong choice for this project, but I wanted to be mobile, intimate, and open to error, something I paid attention to. Candida Höfer's spectacular panoramic library images (which I admire) stand at the opposite end of the spectrum here. Could I accomplish this project with my iPhone today?

I grew up on 1950s American TV, and I remember Jiminy Cricket, little umbrella in hand, doing a number on a bookshelf on *The Mickey Mouse Club,* the towering volumes looming like stage curtains behind the perky character's song and dance. I recalled him roaming around the NLI. Despite their ponderous titles and military formations on the grey metal shelving, books stand mute witnesses to whomever "did it" in any murder scenario. The NLI frequently felt like a prison for books and a few of my images are suggestive of confinement. Several 1960s films physicalized the brain as interior space; *Fantastic Journey* (1966) where a miniaturized team of surgeons travels to a brain resembling bad installation art to laser off a scientist's inoperable tumor. Sometime in 1968, my friend Tom and I went into Manhattan to see the bands Moby Grape and an early Fleetwood Mac with Peter Green. The show was canceled and thus burned (we had advance tickets), we warily ventured Uptown to pre-Midnight-Cowboy-era Times Square into a showing of Kubrick's *2001: A Space Odyssey.* I remember being overwhelmed in my first totally immersive cinema experience. The sequence of the astronaut painstaking dismantling the "brain" of the murderous computer (passive/aggressive great-grand father

---

* David Levi Strauss's *Photography and Belief* (New York: David Zwirner Books, 2020) examines Vilém Flusser's *Towards a Philosophy of Photography* (1983), which posits that that "the camera has a program and most humans are simply functionaries in service to this program."

of Siri) HAL stayed with me, rows of brilliant cassette-like inserts shut down individually to the slurred protests of the regressed machine. I recalled this beautiful scene again moving between floors in the fluorescent gloom of the NLI. This is what memory could look like. Tom hated the movie and advised people waiting in line for the next show not to waste their money.

After spending time in the library I would take my rewound film canisters to be processed at one of Dublin's few professional labs centrally located off of Dame Street. There was a small counter like a take-away manned by several bemused period Dublin hipsters, perhaps students somewhere. I would "put a rush" on my order so I could return to my hotel to examine the slides bending over my luminous little table loop to eye. Imagine this dramatically lit scene from outside my window in Georgian Dublin! There were no problems. We both agree, Catherine, that slides and transparencies are part of a hereditary chain that extends from the proto-photographic/cinema stained-glass window to this very screen. Stained glass is having a revival in contemporary art with Gerhard Richter's Cologne Cathedral window attracting artists to Germany to collaborate with the team of craftsmen he engaged. You held in your hand a sheet of NLI images to the light in our last conversation, Catherine, a grid of 20 slides. Galleries back in the day were inundated by both these reproductions and their holders, and I have many notebooks full of slides endlessly reproduced, each one a little less distinctly from the original, an example of "replica fading," which afflicted the cloned humans in *Blade Runner.* Heritage and seriality.

A lugubrious stained-glass window shines upon the NLI's grand staircase leading directly to somewhere I cannot remember. I photographed the gleaming railing and the functionless curtained pockets of space on either side of the first steps "traps for time" as Robert Smithson once described the interiors of Donald Judd's sculptures. The camera also traps time. I also photographed a segment of the window depicting a book splayed open to reveal pages decorated by shapes resembling loaves or baguettes. No wisdom to be parsed here. A nearby room contained important tomes displayed in cubicles supported by angled luxurious red velvet bases, erotica for the bibliophile.

I never took a book off a shelf. I never brushed accidentally across a fragile, crumbling spine. While I can remember the odor of some things (the Woodstock Festival, art school studios, hospital waiting rooms,) I associate no scent to the NLI. Perhaps, Catherine, we could collaborate on a fragrance, "OLD LIBRARY" by Coty. I returned to NYC and conducted pre-Internet conversations over a selection of images that were printed in Cibachrome from another 4 x 5 in. transparency I would have made. This was costly and being fully reimbursed by the library along with purchasing a set of unique prints that scale (16 x 21 in.) was gratifying. Very few photographic labs print Cibachrome now with the chemistry too toxic to dispose of. In looking back I also take pride that these large bundled prints arrived in Dublin safe and not dented, shipped in a wide metal tube no doubt, benefits from living in proximity to the photo and print industry. I continued to photograph books when I took notice of them and my "career" rode a modest wave of financial gain helped along by representation with a efficient gallery and several positive reviews in major publications. We had no issue with selling multiple prints to decorators and interior designers who in turn supplied corporations and law firms, who I assume recognized the authority and brainy presence of the book image reinforcing the Word As Law. Bookshelves were long the background of morning talk shows and infomercials, making whomever was in front of them appear smart, I guess. Who doesn't check out the bookshelf of some new acquaintance, which could, of course, be slyly contrived decor. (An interior designer friend of mine was given a blank check to purchase coffee-table books for the home of a wealthy Hollywood director—". . . anything to do with French cinema"). A odd by-product of the early weeks of the pandemic was the attention given to "credibility bookcases" in the background of cheery Zoom encounters.

In the 90s, I believed images of books would inhabit a place of nostalgia, but I was wrong; books didn't die although independent bookstores soon may. My students would flock to the annual artist book fair at MoMA PS1 every September, energized by a communal event in contrast to the air-kissing desperation of the art or photo fair. Finally, Catherine, several months ago I reread Umberto Eco's *The Name of The Rose* (1986) in airport-novel paperback form, lurid embossed cover and all. Eco's always been witty, his admission that *Art and Beauty in the Middle Ages* (1985) was written surreptitiously during a stint in the army suggests an Italianate "Sgt. Bilko" barracks life. Eco's sleuth, Brother William of Baskerville, was a monk from the British Isles, who like Sherlock Holmes in *The Hounds of the Baskervilles* (1901–2) periodically disappears in the course of his investigation(s) to let his "Watson" do some digging of his own in the maze-like hallucination-inducing library. As a whodunit written by a medievalist and noted semiotician, it was a hit with both the intelligentsia (especially artists I knew) and the general public. However "who" actually did it is not easily grasped as an ensuing altercation burns the entire monastery to the ground in a dramatic firestorm. The story begun with our now elderly "Watson" returning to the overgrown ruin to retrieve a fragment of text now ash, which ignites the tale. In *A Scandal in Bohemia* (1891), Holmes would don a disguise to recover a compromising photograph when images represented the indisputable truth, maybe the first featured role of a photograph in popular fiction.

Most art objects are made to be looked at, a few to be "read." Words are introduced on or into the object/image or available in the form of a explanatory label usually adjacent to the art's current location. Texts are information and all information is poetry—"concrete" poetry found disordered throughout the shelves of the NLI to be flattened, reproduced and sequenced inside the cameras' blind interior. Clicking through these picture now (as the season changes behind me) there are two I wish to bring your final attention and response. One is of a desktop computer, I enlarge the picture to discover it's an IBM PS/1 (!) available to navigate the collection with its own compressed microchip library, an eager to please little servant unlike the paranoid HAL. Is the mildly smarmy description "user friendly" still in use? The final image I click on is a green-leather-ribbony blur, a library collapse or fainting spell, I purposefully shook the camera setting the bookshelves ablaze. I would hope that this picture would sound how it looks.

Tim Maul
03/14/21

Tim Maul and Catherine Morris

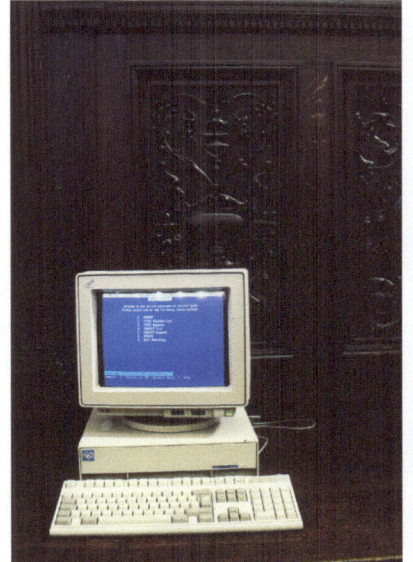

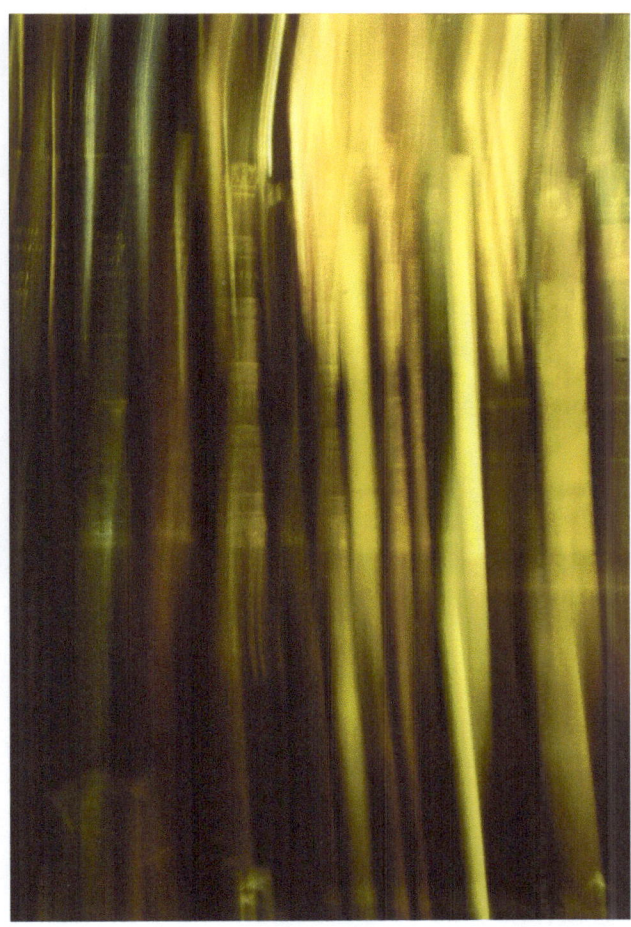

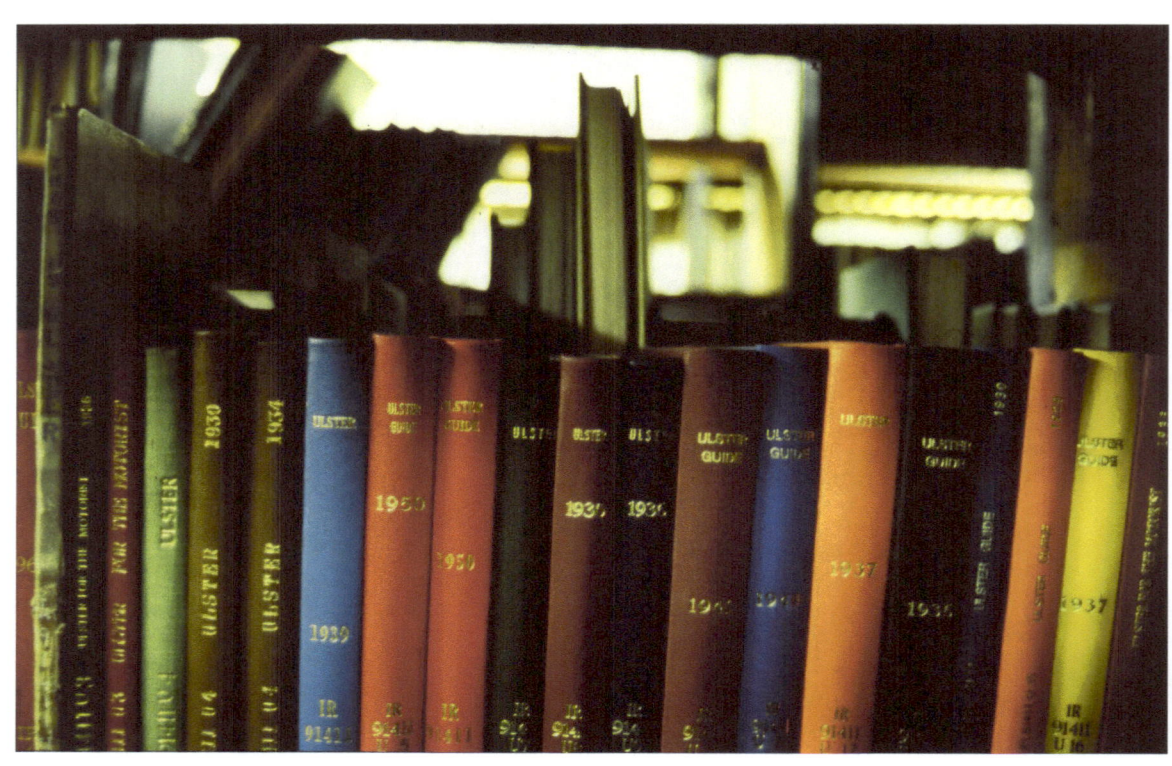

I

1930
1934
Ulster
1937

IR91411v39
Saunders Political Reformers

II

Visconti
1806 Volume I

gold
tiring in the late afternoon's
shade to night

1887 almost out of view
I want to take another left go the
other way—

No. Stay here thinking about
Italian Marxism
Visconti

not Ulster 1937

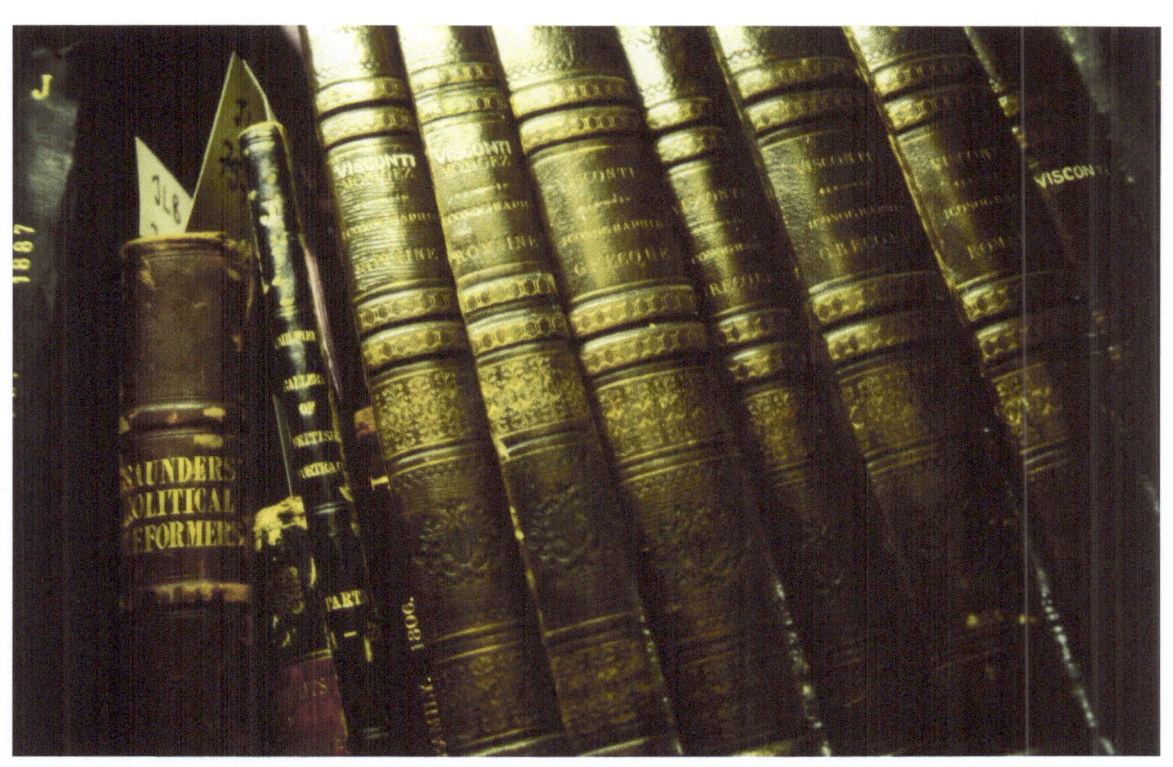

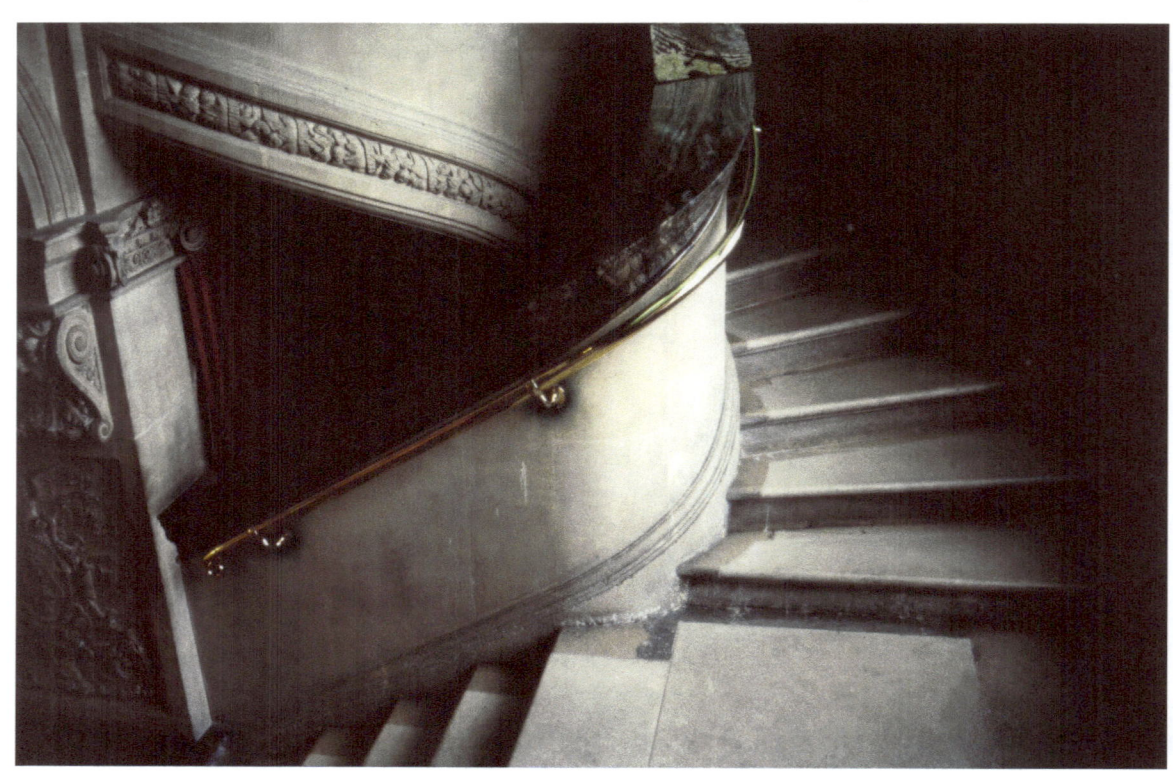

III

Curving spine of
whispered conversations
That moment in time fixed in
decorative stone fruit
I emerge from the Reading Room

Microfilm of state secrets
vertigo falling inside me
a moment of a story
taking shape
my daughter is somewhere growing

Out in to the night
I stumble onto
Kildare street

IV

Touching glass
An open book
an invitation.
Joe Westmoreland and I
Walked up and in
through darkness.
The silence of
that closed library
the archive breathes us in;
snow outside.
A lover's bed in
New York City
The boys curled up on Merce Cunningham's chair.
We walk a cinematic line to see Lori.
Charles' coffee cold in the fridge ready for morning.
Ice on the High Line and Catherine in pink
looking out at the stage
the spectator
active not passive.

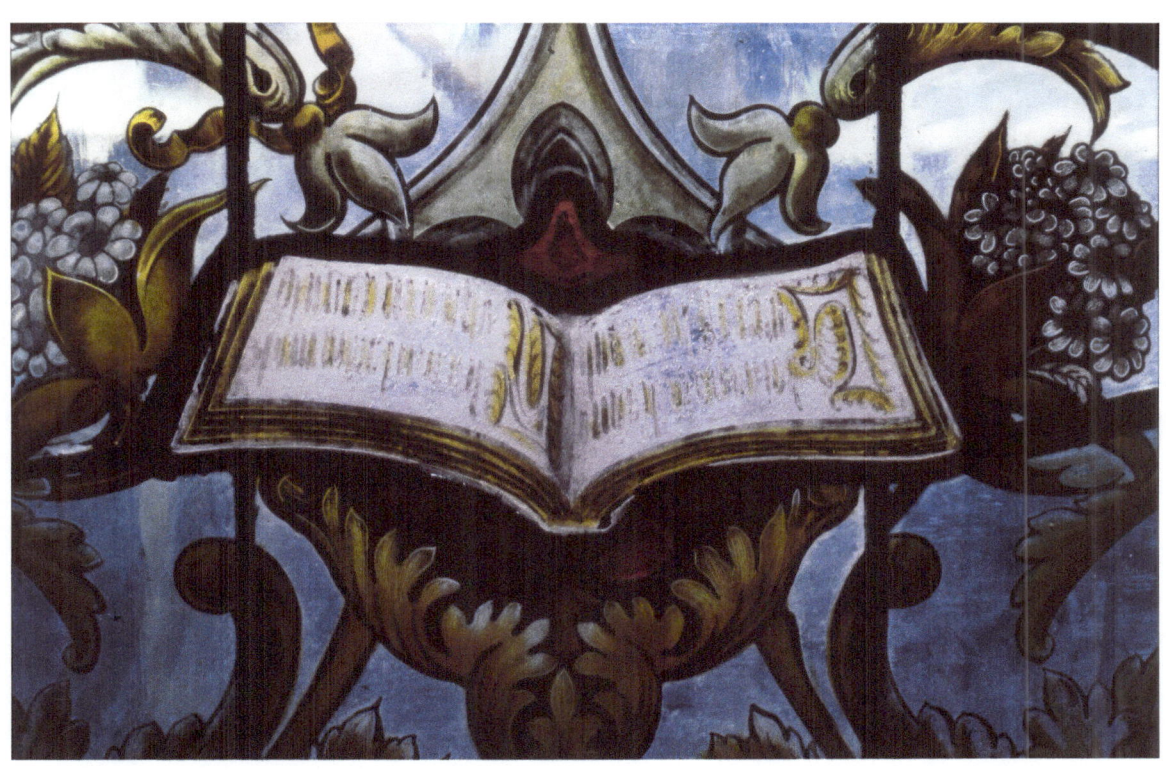

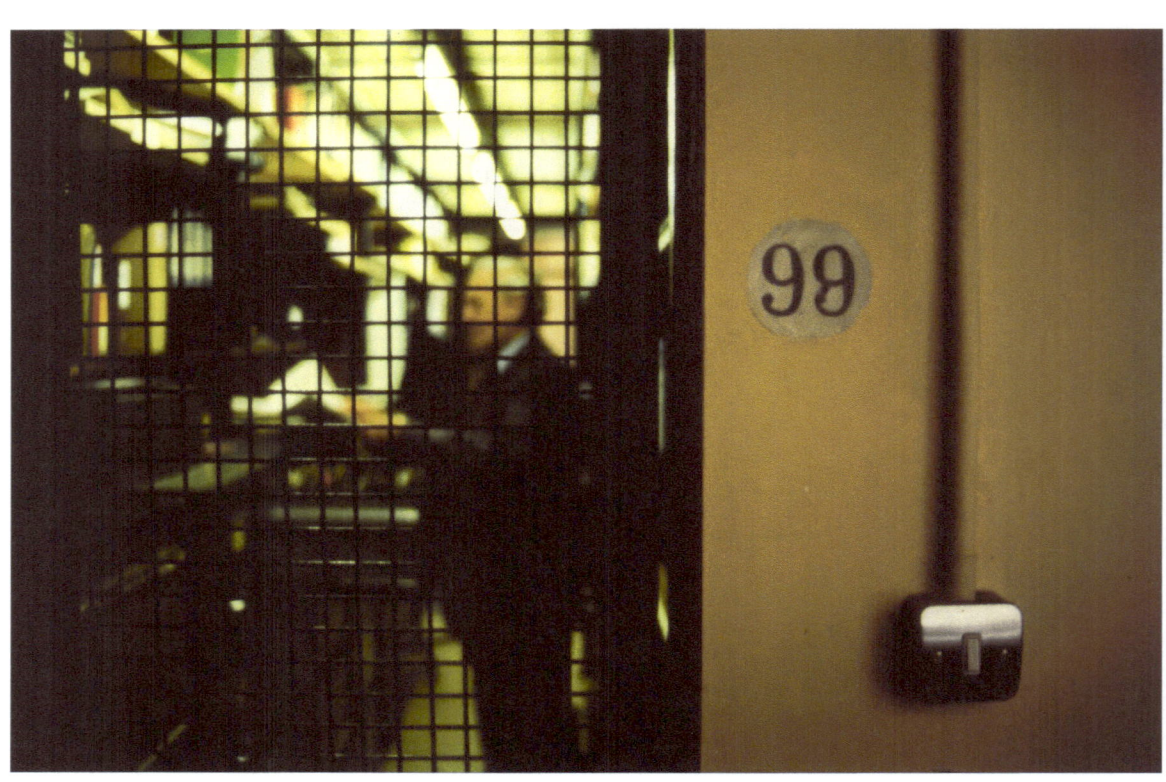

V

It was my sister who
told them about my brother...
my father...my—

So many betrayals
behind the Iron Curtain.
That neon light
A journey past Visconti
Ulster 1937
Into fragments

a glass page
Nicaragua, Cambodia, Myanmar, the Uighurs in forced labour camps
Pages   documents
Evidence of:
What she said
Who he saw
How the state and
multinationals confused
the algorithms

fragments
left
torn somehow

VI

Gold slides down her face
and onto her shoes
Larks in the Parks
Sefton Park
back to the 80s again.
Liverpool again.

Is this a painting?
a glance behind a curtain?
An angel's wing
flown in from
Ethiopia
Russia?

That room in the
National Gallery
a breath away

I think of you Tim
what did you say about Richter?

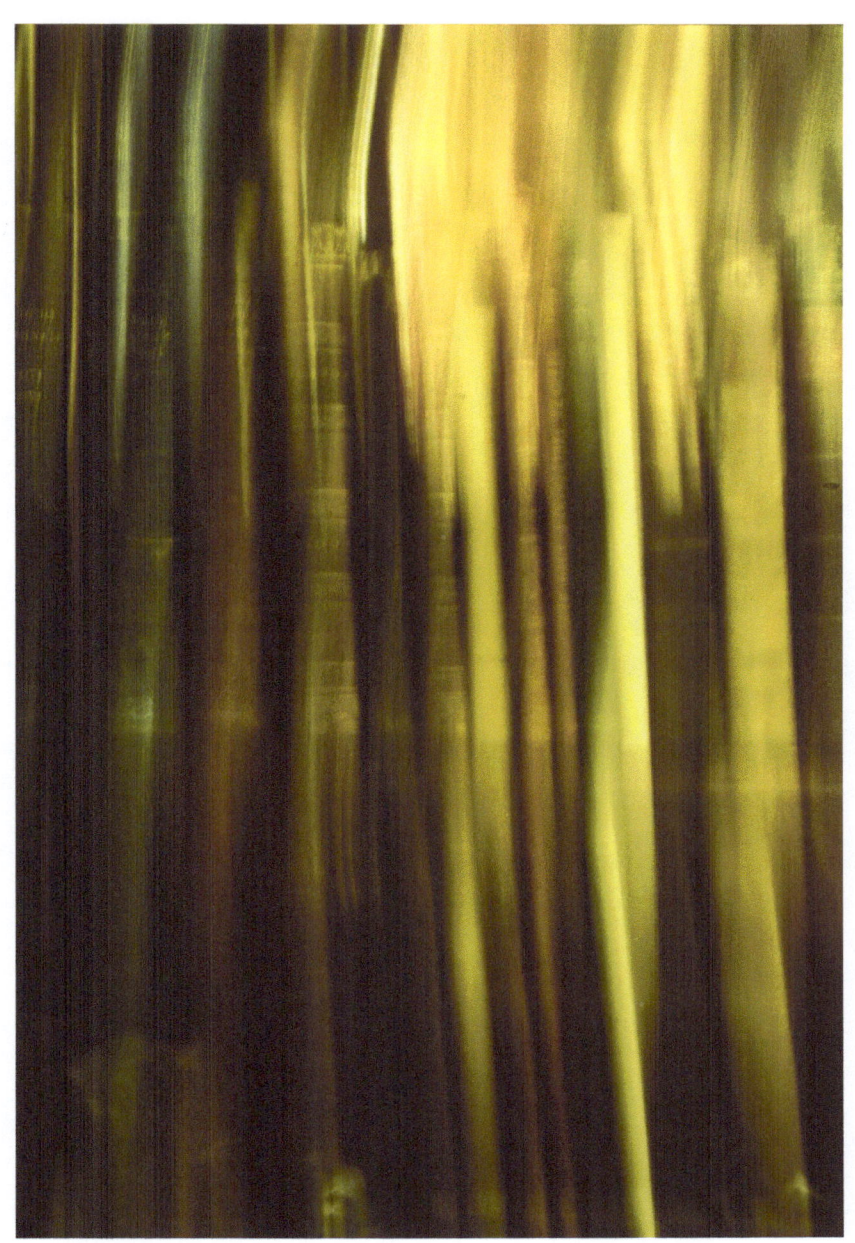

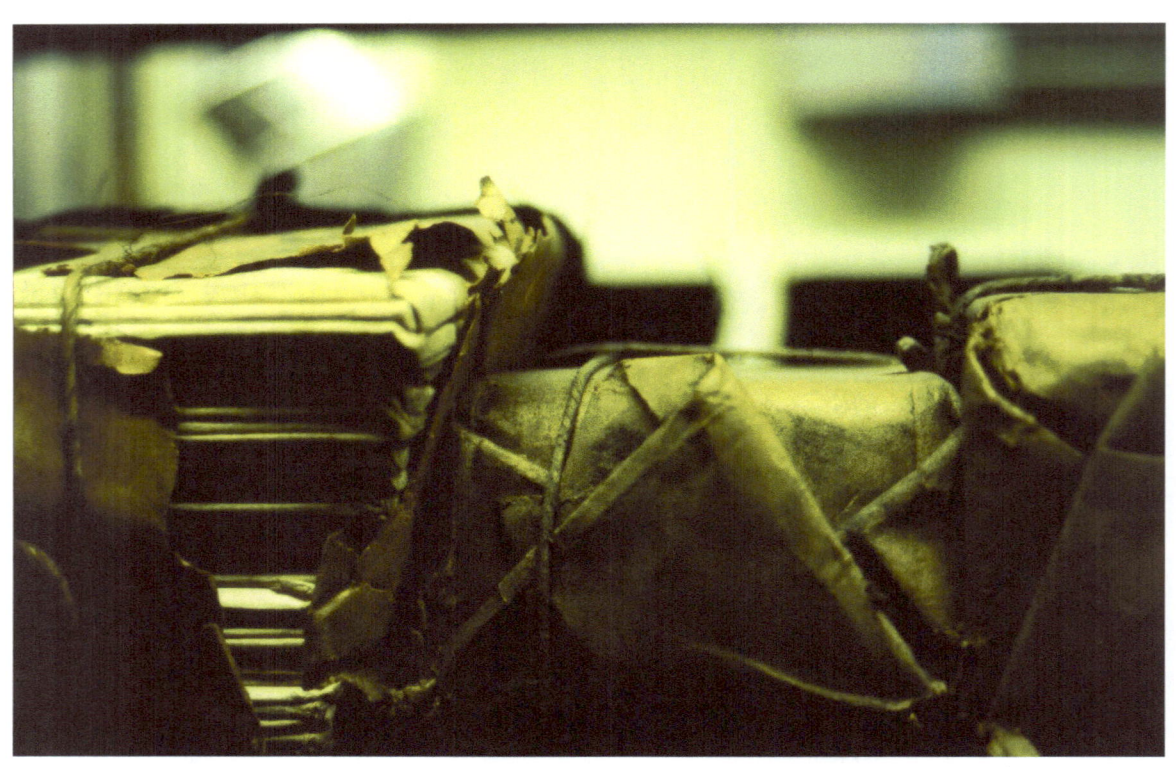

VII

String
folds into
a triangle
that holds the war

paper covers
holds
breaks in time
life lines
song birds
that half light
another darkness that does not hesitate

VIII

Meath Show Catalogue
Munster Show Catalogue
1940
Munster Agricultural Society

1932–34

808—IR 0305m9
"Missing numbers," is what they'd
say at the desk—
everything now has to be pre-ordered
the art of getting lost
disappeared
while they were sleeping

—the most valuable part of the city, she thinks.

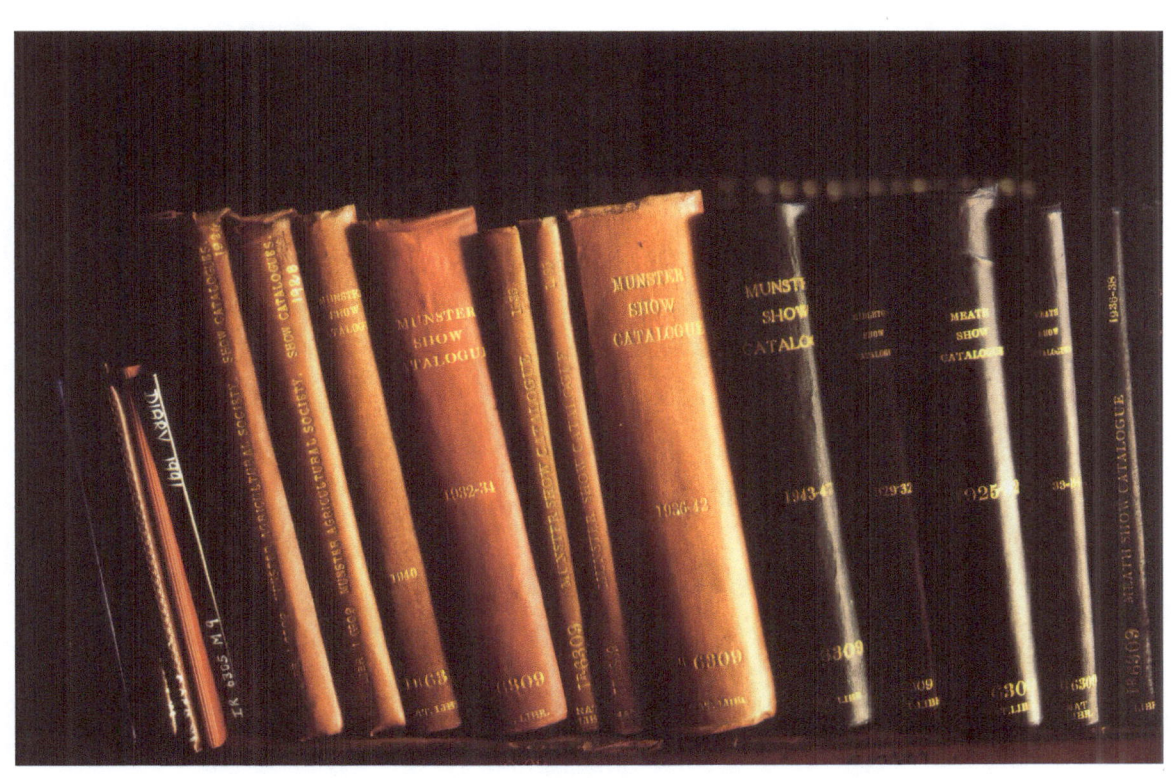

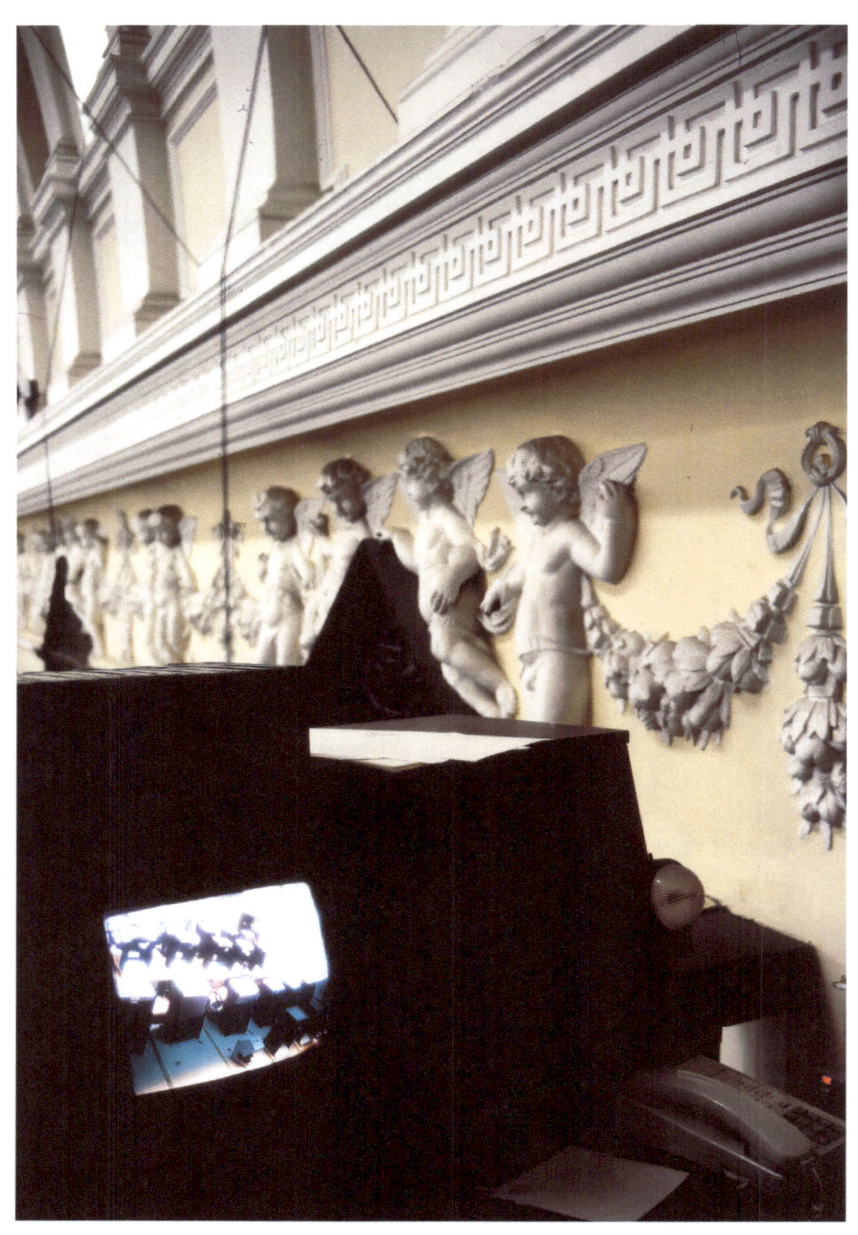

IX

Children higher than they should be
More silent than they should be
Wearing less clothes than they should wear

Plaster angels pinned to the high walls
of the Reading Room
Reading our thoughts as sentences
feeling lost desires
circulate up and out
through the day
Mondays 9am—9pm—any days 9am—9pm
"They are the best days," she thinks.

Angels' eyes watch our redirections
fade and reappear as years
The tv monitor watching
what?
A telephone that does not ring.

X

The grey of a computer
Blue screen white letters
It is this not the library that was in its death throws, thinks Catherine.
A way to search books beyond
Hard-back pages
of glued-in hand-written
references
the elegance of being
something more beautiful than we are

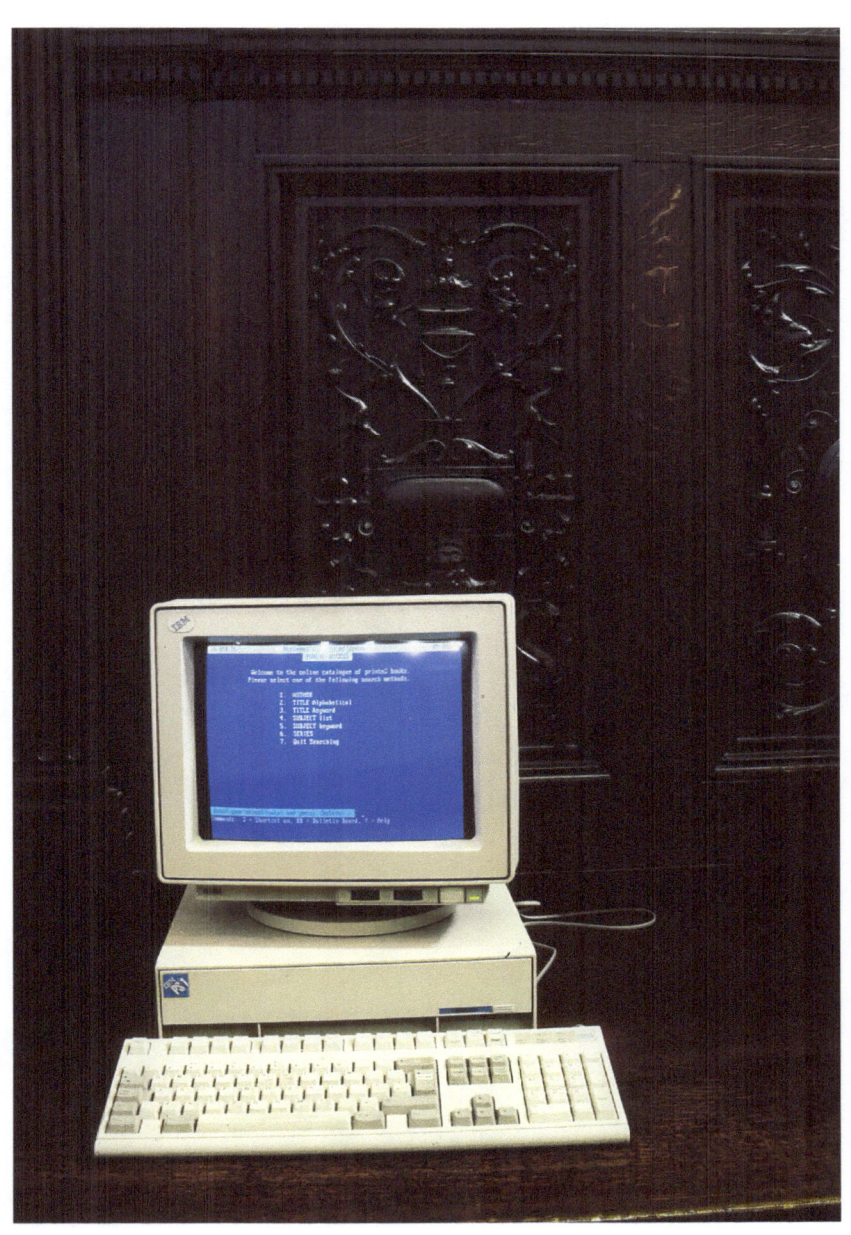

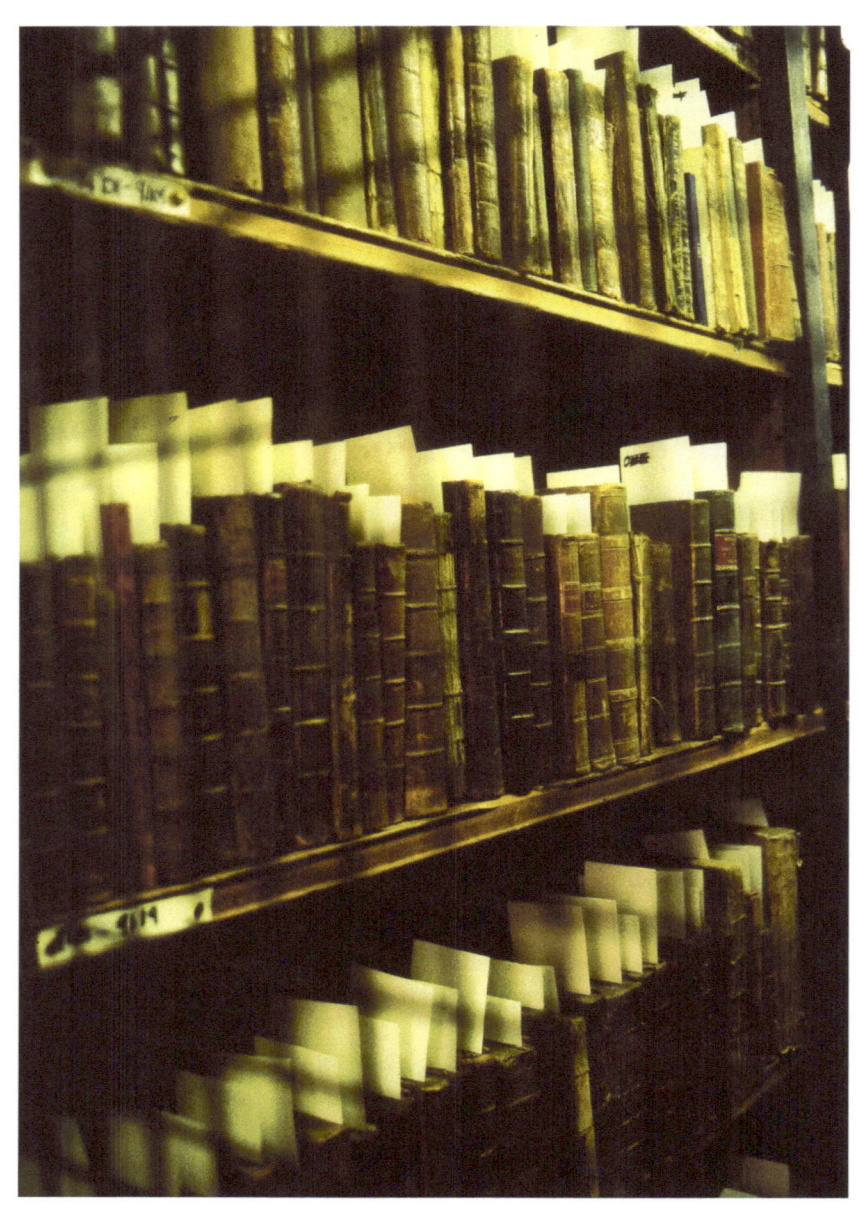

XI

White burning into
regulating
broken spines

hidden

stories

XII

And now I see the ghost
that you had seen in 1986
that woman disappearing
for twenty thirty forty years
standing in the shadows of
solidarity
the kindness of workers
that lasts forever

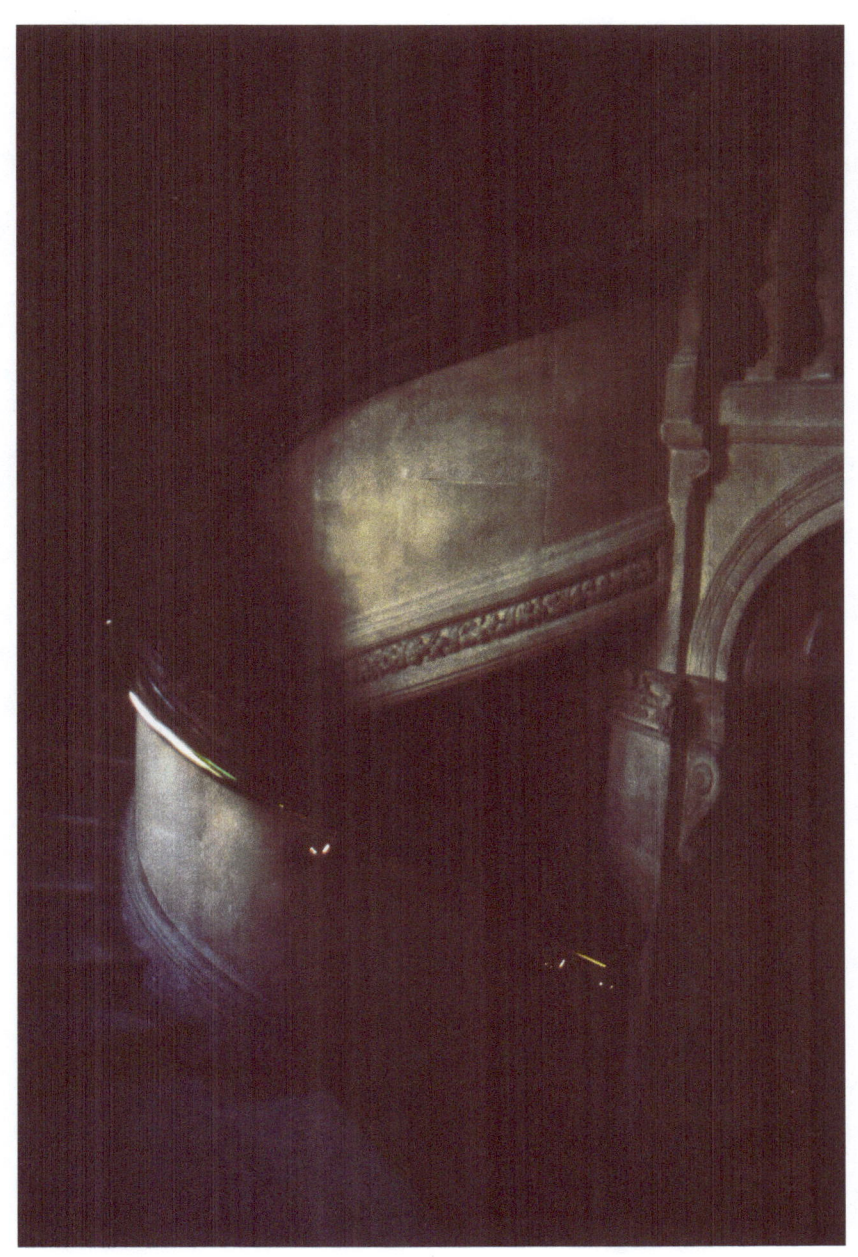

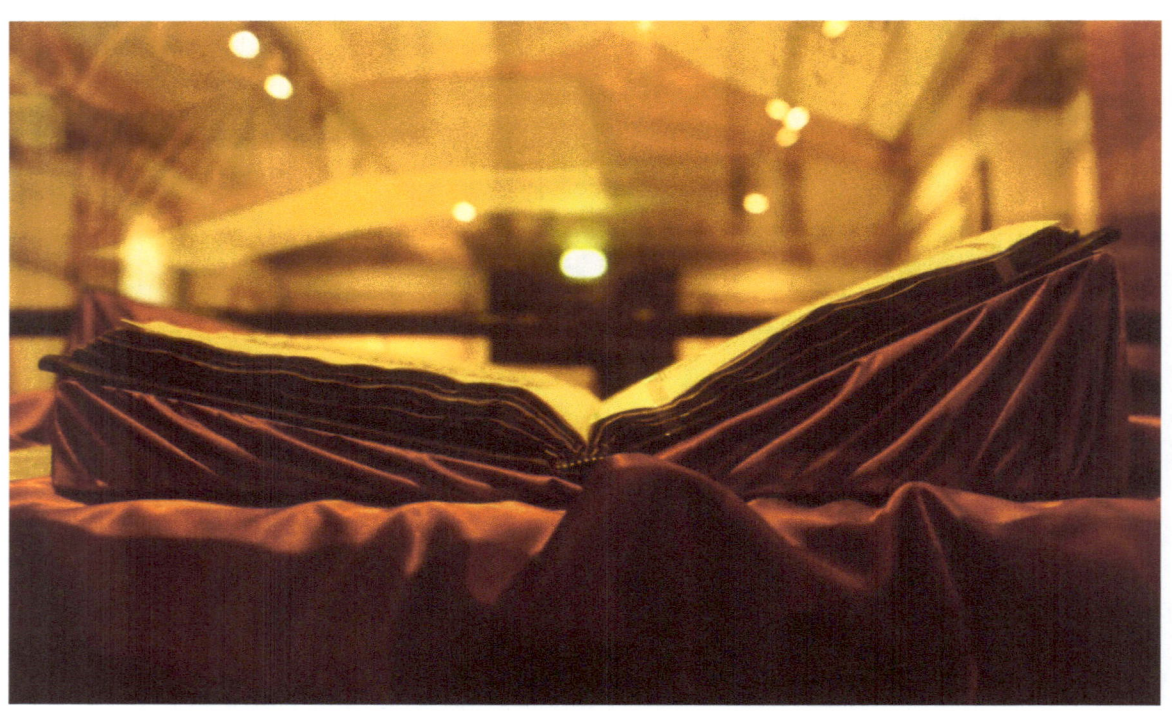

XIII

Ulysses
Molly Bloom
red
rose rose slowly sank red rose. Heartbeats: her breath

I'd confuse him a little alone with him if we were Id let him see my

make him turn red looking at him seduce him

XIV

"Sugradh"
What does that mean?
I'll ask Mairead
at the St Patrick's Day
Dora Maar
as new bird song
finds its way through
our broken lives
the church made
unhealed wounds
across the wall
from where I write.

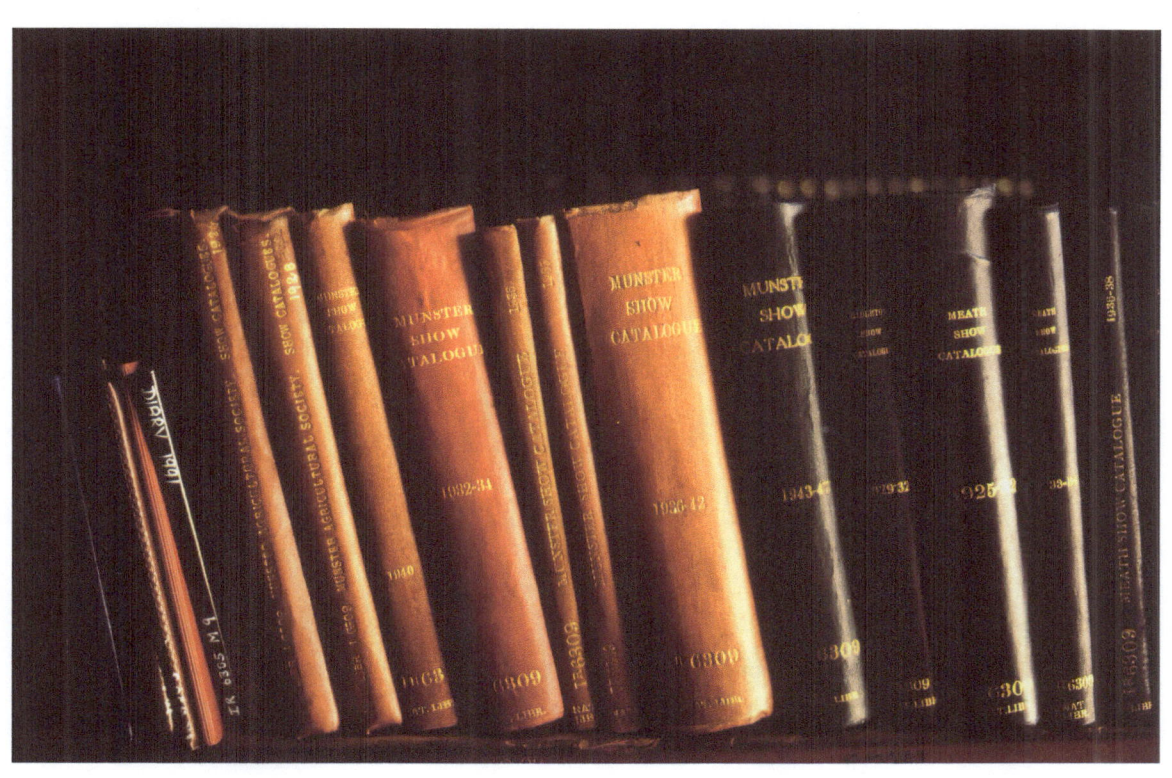

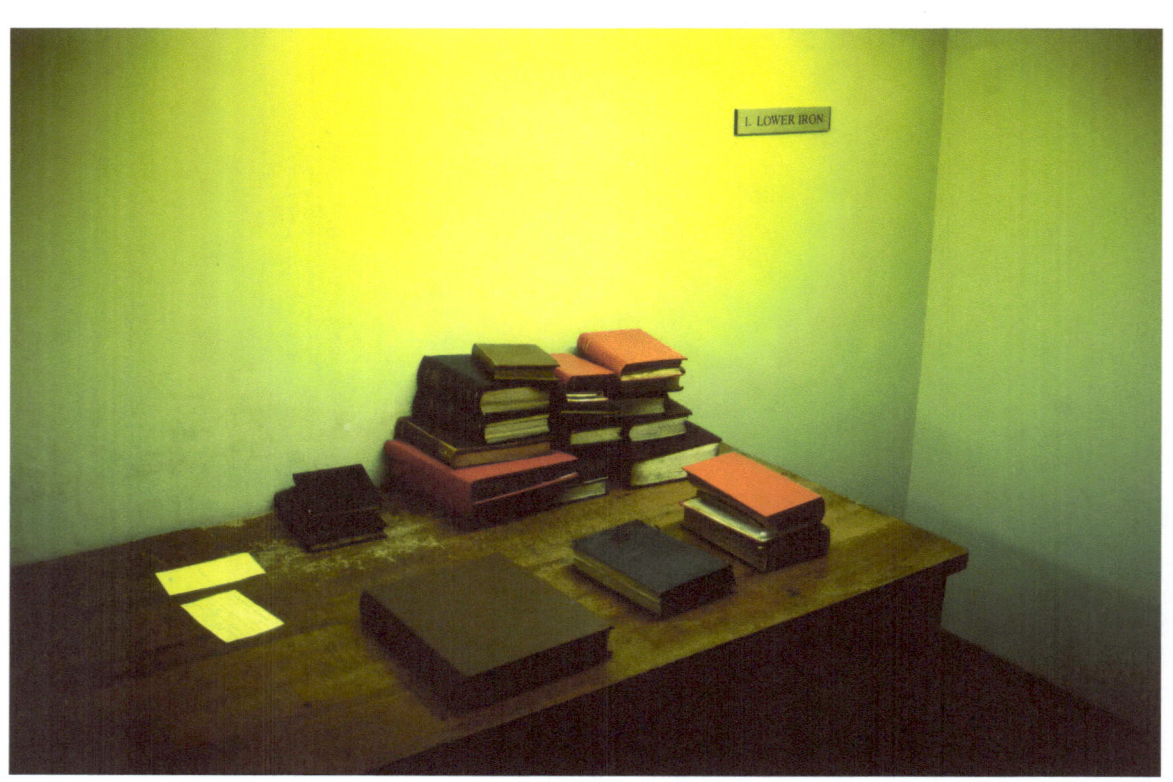

XV

I wanted to know
what I did not ask
Language formed
words that came
too late

"You did nothing wrong," the Taoiseach said in his State apology.
She watched herself
step
over a car
in Belfast
body parts
burnt out in the
long ago

So usual they
had become as
invisible as the disappeared
absent from view
as a stack of anonymised
books placed on a
wooden table
against a yellow wall
beneath a sign that reads
I. Lower Iron

XVI

Reading writing here
in the company of
electronic distance
I hear seagulls
fly into the Claddagh
You hear the silence
of a city in pandemic
where bird sound finds itself.

That open door in the Reading Room
always too hot or too cold
1986—the Miners knew
the archive would
store
vindicate
what they had said and saw and
what "we" all knew.
Vindication of the Rights of Women
That will take longer, she thought.

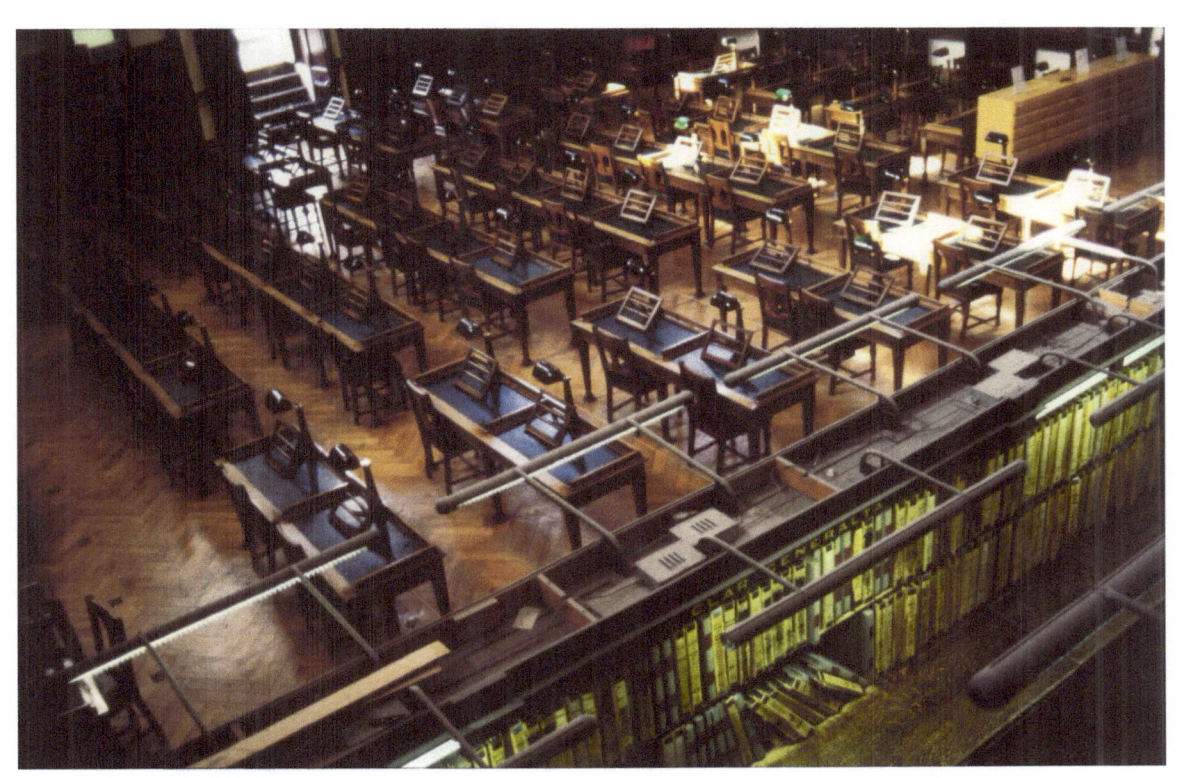

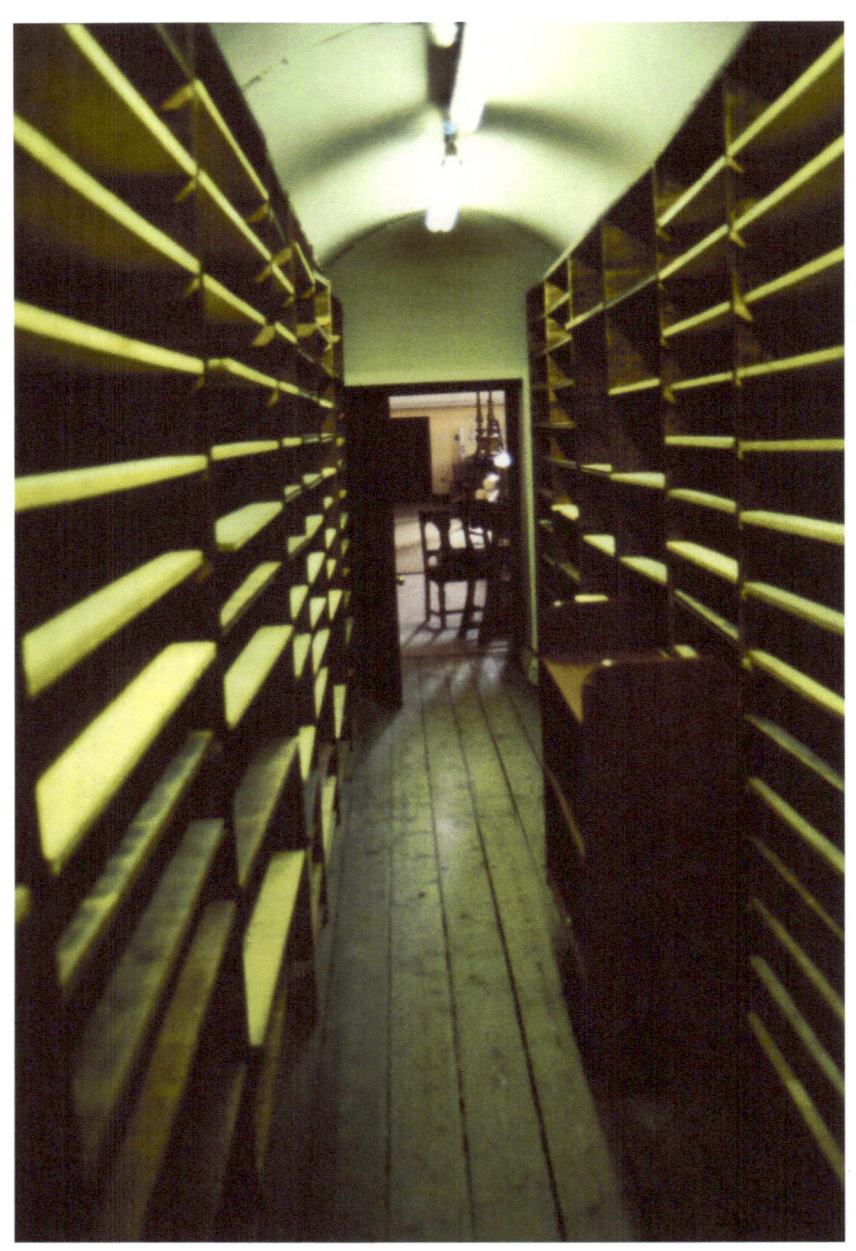

XVII

A shape
of direction
the strip

light falls
on the edges
of
a door to enquiry.

You standing there.

Through that open door
on that empty shelf

did you see what
it was about
your mother
you had come
here to find?—

XVIII

They did something with his
coffin and I went "home"

to an attic room
high above a city
that glanced
the memory of itself through the
windows of a museum

That night after the funeral
I bled out my life and
turned the mattress
like a ritual
soil tilled in a field eyes lifting to the sun
a picture stolen by Nazis
framed on a Parisienne gallery wall
for too long
it was seen

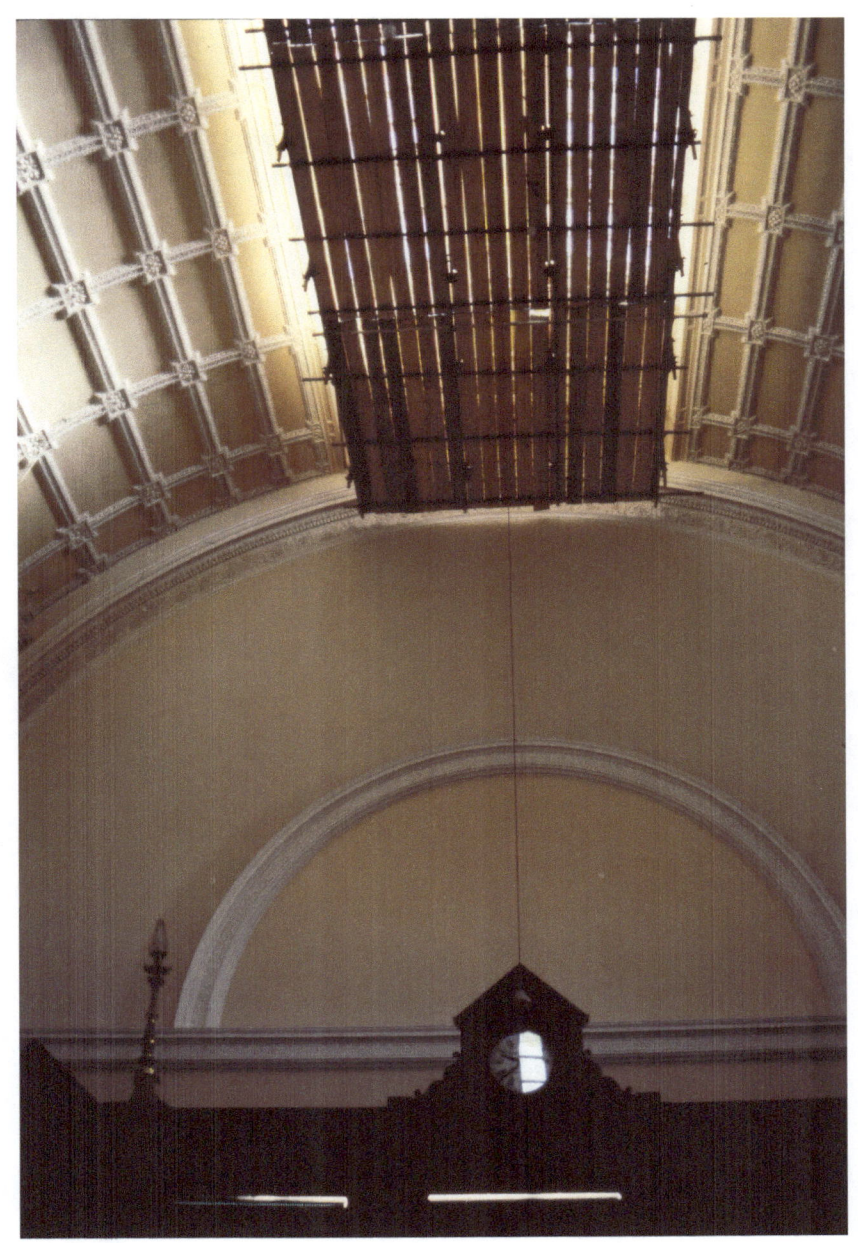

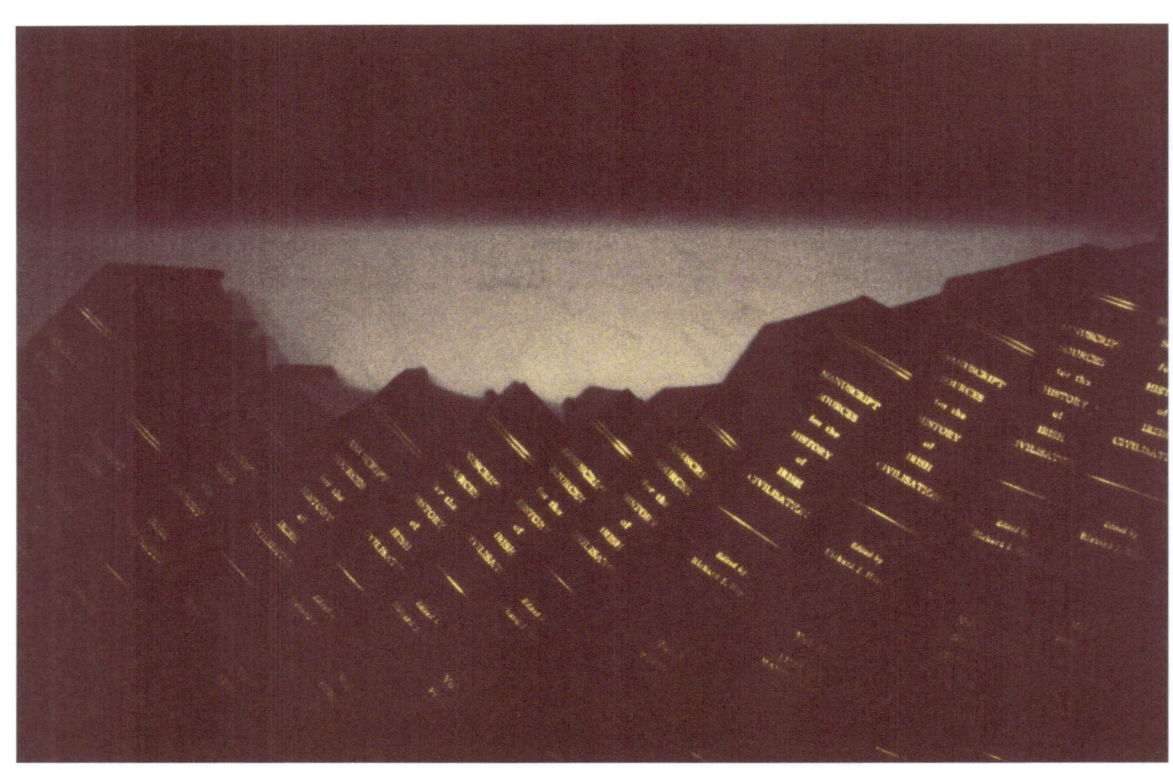

XIX

Lying down
aching in love
leaning into
the gaze of
each other
hurt by the changes
that the Hunger Strikers cannot effect

Bodies   Books
listening close
to the corridors of
the State
where power
does and does not
reside
Manuscript Sources for the History of
Irish Civilisation.

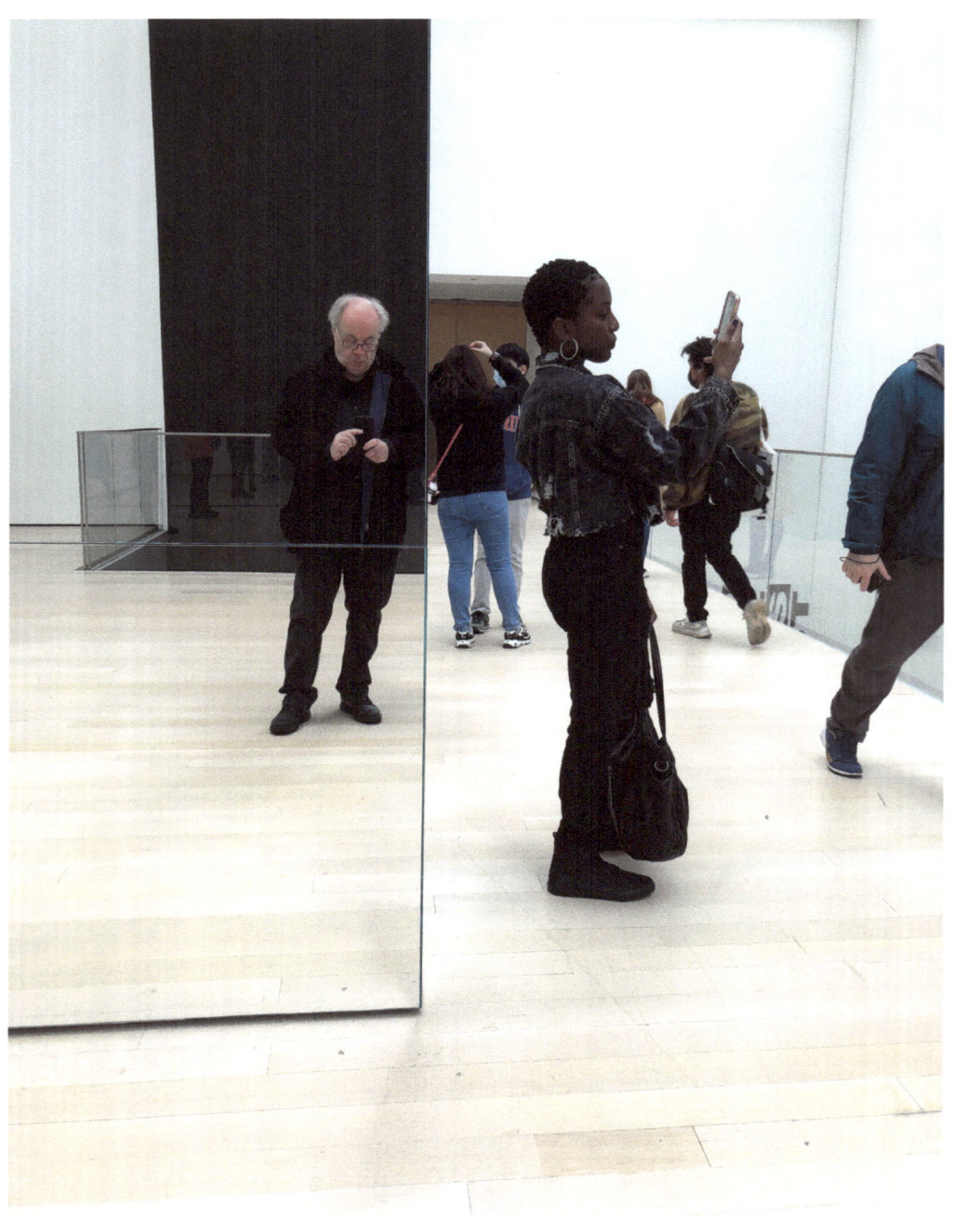

Coda

March 3, 2023

A) In the summer of 2020, Catherine Morris and I agreed to develop a writing project around a set of 35mm slides I had gifted her from my 1994 commission with the National Library of Ireland. We wanted to attempt an image/writing exchange outside of the positivist "creative" busywork that appeared early in the ongoing pandemic. (I ponder what an "Art of the Pandemic" exhibition might look like and recall an 80s curator friend sharing with me that it's "not the art but the names involved"). Our first ZOOM feels like a long time ago, and a few things have changed. My texting, for one, is nimbler now, often punctuated with images resembling the brainy art I thought I would make in the 70s. Catherine, rereading AFTERMATH I hear the rich Anglo-Irish intonations of your voice ("Ah") and also mine, who I am told sounds like my brother Michael who died over the phone, quarantined at Yale in New Haven around a month before we began. His was an autistic voice, urgent and inquiring. He loved libraries and visited the Stamford Public Library every weekday of his adult life. He pored over almanacs, "who's who," and anything with numbers. I accompanied him once (he preferred being alone), and he entered the building like an archaeologist entering a tomb. Perhaps this was the approach I took photographing the NLI that soggy week in 90s Dublin. We intersect here, Catherine, unknown to me you studied and toiled in this building while Tim in cub-reporter mode, camera at the ready, sought a scoop among the shelves, a body maybe, and I believe I found one (AFTERMATH) in this labyrinthian "mind palace."* For

> * A term used by Benedict Cumberbatch's Sherlock Holmes for his vast storage facility of a memory. Let's admit here that Mark Gaddis and Stephen Moffat blew it with the "Jim Moriarty" character on the series *Sherlock* (2010–17) brilliantly portrayed by the Dubliner and "out" actor Andrew Scott. Conan Doyle's Professor Moriarty, a gentleman deviant and the "Napoleon of Crime" surely represented the worst possible social manifestation of the Irish in Victorian London.

the coda Klaus Ottmann requested we also agreed to write about each other's image (the authors!) by sharing "selfies." Mine was taken exiting the Wolfgang Tillmann's MoMA retrospective last fall. I'm glad I went, there were many big pictures to see. Tillmann's "owns" the salon-style presentation of casually affixed prints still prevalent in photo department exhibitions. But I wasn't alone in detecting a undercurrent of loss threading through this immersive tsunami of precise, unsentimental images of youth culture in a euphoric Europe before the millennium and Brexit. I was unaware that he was HIV positive. At the exit you were confronted with a big mirrored cube like a giant Robert Morris (!) piece from the 60s, a selfie magnet that affirms something in people, but what? Tell me. (There is a strong possibility that mirrors were covered in my Irish Grandmother's home in Connecticut after a death in '63 so that her departing spirit would not be confused as to where to go. Tillman's cube covered would resemble the Kaaba in Mecca).

B) In the image you provided me you are captured twice, first digitally by your iPhone, and for a second time in the glass of a wooden cabinet, somewhat askew. A tiny letter in the upper right hand corner indicates that it's cabinet "D." We're in surreal waters here; Marcel Duchamp appreciated shop window displays and produced one for the Gotham Book Mart where I whiled away many a lunch hour in the 80s. But I choose to locate you in a delirious version of one of Joseph Cornell's boxes, who, if Carl Andre is correct, is the source of Pop Art via Rauschenberg and, later, Warhol. You are in safer (albeit clammy) hands here than with, say, Man Ray. There is a pillar to your left and it's unclear whether you are in or out of doors, but wait, the floor! Your coat looks both warm and smart. There is evidence that the cabinet's glass may have hosted posters or announcements by the remnants of tan shipping tape. Your eyes are either masked or blindfolded by a floating red band, and your iPhone is covered by four additional vertical lengths of tape. I remembered that you had bangs like Alice Liddell, a notorious photographer's subject whose possible surrogate famously traveled through mirrors *ad infinitum.* There is a direct lineage from fictional Alice to Duchamp's "Bride" sealed between two sheets of intricately repaired glass accom-

panied by a green edition of prismatic occult language.** Plate glass
(and the medium of photography) was in usage in the 1870s offering
dreams money can buy and attracting the consumptive gaze of urban
"flaneurs" in major Western cities. Cornell haunted Manhattan "window
shopping" in his seemingly endless free time. There is also a trace of
photographer Francesca Woodman present, a tragic 20th century Romantic figure cherished by students held in permanent suspension between
adolescence and adulthood, occasionally frozen in a manic blur of her
own making. Victoriana aside, what clearly signaled your attention was
that this cabinet contained stacks of books in a horizontal piles like
bodies in a football game, or worse, atrocity corpses. (Are libraries
where books go to die?) The titles on the spines are mostly readable,
ornately embossed several in gold and with patterns. Your reflected form
is stenciled with marvelously appropriate language-"engraving" or your
forehead, "Art," "Portraits," and across your middle section "The Lake
Scenery of England." This slippage between designated object and name
is a familiar one originating with Magritte's "Pipe" (surrealism again)
through to mostly everything of Jasper Johns. In this moment scholar,
poet, and library mesh in the magic space that cinema, waiting in the
wings, was about to exploit. "USE DISSOLVES" advised Godard.***

** In 1912, Duchamp passed an examination that earned him a librarian position
at the Bibliotheque Sainte-Genevieve which he thoroughly enjoyed. As a student
(1972–73) of Kynaston McShine we discussed the "aura" of autism around both
Duchamp and Warhol in relation to my brother.

*** Godard also said that "Mirrors should reflect before sending an image."

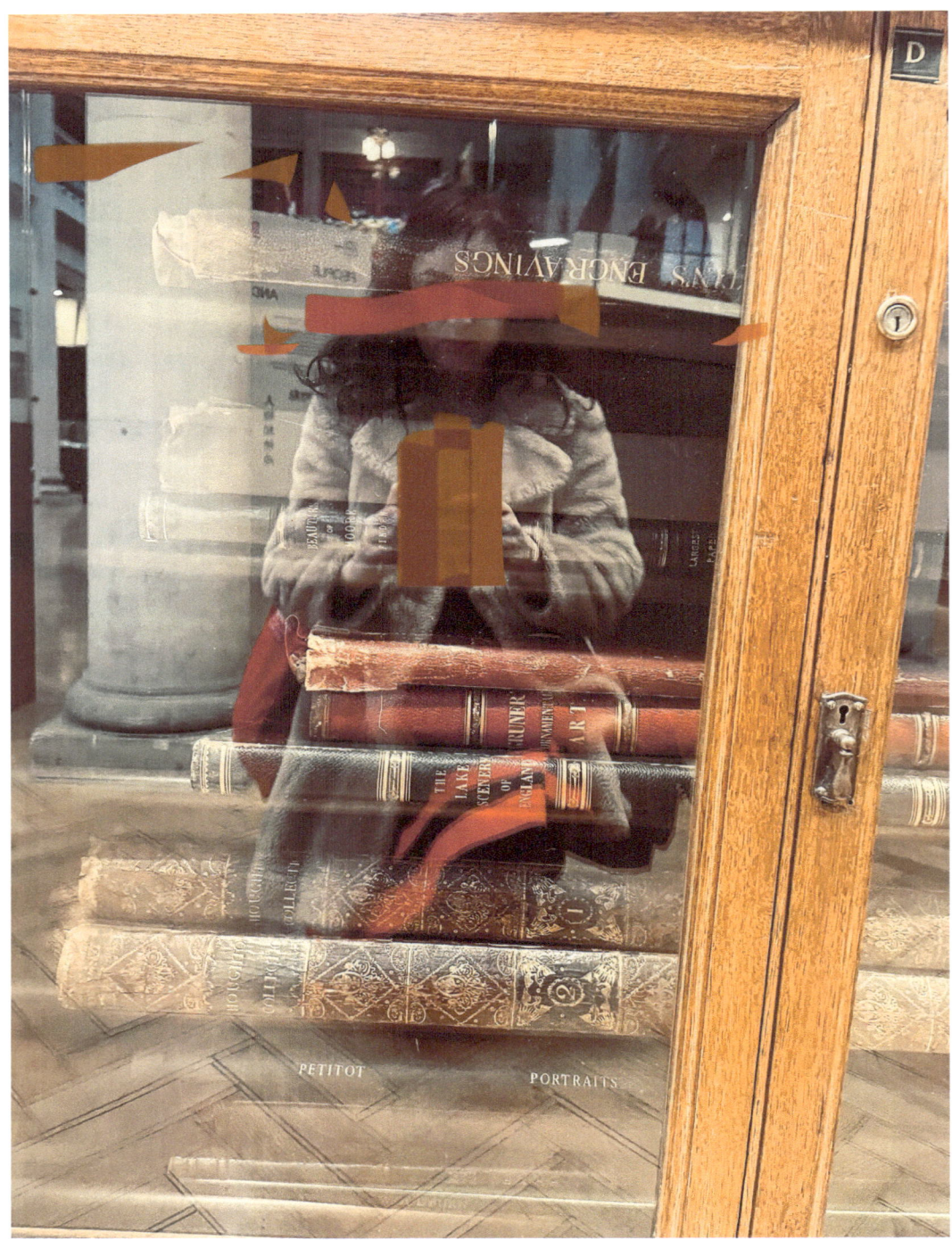

A nineteenth century villa that is taller than the seven trees that surround it, four terraced streets named after Irish villages, St Michael-in-the-Hamlet's cast iron pillars, a supermarket delivery van, and my mind's desiring block my view of the River Mersey this morning.

Olga Tokarczuk said: "Being imagined is the first stage in existence."

Short exchanges that transform invisible days into feeling.

In 2022, my father and then a close friend of mine died; bookends made of sandstone fell off both ends of my year. I throw the torn fragments of my unspoken funeral orations into the Mersey and wait for the tide to turn. On Sunday as I lay in bed, the absolute consequence of their forever absence was all over this city.

To be both. We are both back in March 2020. Your last exchange with your brother down a hospital phone line. My last words sung with my mother and father down a phone line from Galway to a care home in Liverpool. Walking through the university on the west coast of Ireland everything slows to empty. An emergency sounding out to sea; people disappeared. In this aftermath I read back through the archive: the silence that I stepped into was a last time. I pass the black shining counter where a year before I had left a bunch of flowers I did not want to receive: "please take."

Over the months of the pandemic what was it that was broken? Something more intimate than the historic journey etched into my parents' post-war lives of concerted freedom.

You wrote that in taking photographs in the National Library on your Nikon: "For this journey I wanted to be mobile, intimate, and open to error. Something I paid attention to." I read your lines this morning and think about what was taken from me when I was cut open in 1989, and I wonder what part of Catherine was left.

Mobile
intimate
open to error.
Something
I pay attention to.

Our conversation finds its shape in archive; the curve of that servant tunnel in Strokestown where you did not want to stay for too long. I hear the voices of those Famine Refugees lose themselves again in Irish on the docks in Liverpool. Following your own footsteps back through the National Library you say:

"This is what memory could look like."

Catherine on a Monday in March 2023 thinks: on this day a hundred years ago the Irish did and did not settle for Partition, and women who opposed the Free State were imprisoned by their first republic. Tim writes: "The camera also traps time."

TIM MAUL is an artist and art writer based in New York City and Connecticut. He is represented by Florence Loewy in Paris and Leslie Tonkonow Artworks + Projects in New York. Institutional collections include The Metropolitan Museum of Art in New York and the Centre Georges Pompidou in Paris.

CATHERINE MORRIS is a writer, academic and editor. Her monograph *Alice Milligan and the Irish Cultural Revival* (Four Courts Press, 2012) uncovered the forgotten cultural feminist arts practice of one of the founders of modern Ireland. She is currently Senior Lecturer in Creative Writing & Literature at Liverpool Hope University.

Published by Spring Publications
Thompson, Conn.
www.springpublications.com

First edition 2023

Cover image:

Tim Maul
Saint Agatha's Seen from Charleville Road, Dublin, 2022
Digital photograph

ISBN: 978-0-88214-141-1 (e-book edition, 1.1)

Library of Congress Control Number: 2023938140